D1545554

Rare Books
and
Royal Collectors

MEMOIRS OF AN

ANTIQUARIAN BOOKSELLER

BY

Maurice L. Ettinghausen

Simon and Schuster
New York
1966

"On ne doit jamais écrire que de ce qu'on aime. L'oubli et le silence sont la punition qu'on inflige à ce qu'on a trouvé laid ou commun, dans la promenade à travers la vie."

—RENAN, *Souvenirs d'enfance et de jeunesse*

Preface

*Before the end of the Second World War I was
asked by the secretary of the Oxford University Society of Bibliophiles to give the members a talk on
some of my experiences. This society, which consisted chiefly of undergraduates but with a few senior
members, meets periodically during termtime and is,
as a rule, hospitably received at a final meeting
(when their latest acquisitions are displayed) by Mr.
John Sparrow, the Warden of All Souls', and treated
to hot punch in his lovely rooms.*

*A couple of years ago I was asked by the English
Jewish Historical Society in London to give them a
talk on some of my reminiscences. Since then my
sons and some of my grandchildren have been urging
me to write out some of my book experiences more
fully.*

*I have also been encouraged in this by Mr. M.
Lincoln Schuster, of Simon and Schuster (my publishers), who wrote me in the spring of 1964 from
New Delhi that he was interested in my plan. He
wrote:*

*"I am sure you know a celebrated best-seller about
forty years ago,* The Amenities of Book-Collecting,

7

by the late A. Edward Newton, of Philadelphia. You might well consider trying to get the same tone of voice, the same spirit, and the same colorful details that will make the book appeal not only to other professional collectors and antiquarians. A technical work on this subject would have a certain but limited appeal, i.e., to other collectors and specialists on rare and old books. But a book that takes the intelligent representative nonprofessional reader behind the scenes, at the summit, so to speak, could have a considerably larger audience."

I am afraid I have not tried to carry out Mr. Schuster's suggestions. I have not tried to imitate any other autobiography; I have simply jotted down my rambling reminiscences. I have deliberately omitted any scandal or detraction of reputations. I have not given the story of the Spanish professor of chemistry who came to see me at the Ritz Hotel, Madrid, asking me for a list of books I might wish to buy, and informing me that during the summer vacation he would be visiting many public libraries where he was sure to find these books. When I indignantly objected to his uninvited presence in my room he replied, "But I always take out the library stamps, just as I am doing for the most eminent local collectors"! I told him to get out or I would throw him down the stairs.

There are many other stories that I could have told to the discredit of eminent persons, but such stories should be told, if at all, in minute detail and in full context, for proper understanding. Amusing stories—even about bibliophiles—may be told in such casual memoirs as mine, but I have neither the time nor the inclination to dwell on unpleasantness.

On July 20, 1920, the Empress Eugénie, widow of the Emperor Napoleon III, was buried near her home at Farnborough, the funeral being attended by King George V and Queen Mary, King Alfonso of Spain and Queen Ena, King Manuel of Portugal and Queen Victoria. Among the mourners was Prince Victor Napoleon, grandson of Napoleon's youngest brother, Jerome, King of Westphalia. His father (nicknamed "Plon Plon") was a nephew of the Emperor Napoleon and had been renowned during the Second Empire as an extreme radical, in spite of the fact that he was married to Princess Clothilde, the youngest daughter of Victor Emmanuel II of Italy. He had been a minister in Napoleon III's governments and played an important part during the Emperor's reign.

Prince Victor Napoleon,* who was present at the Farnborough funeral, had not been on good terms with his father; he was forbidden, when his father lay dying in a Roman hotel in 1891, to come to his deathbed—even though he was the claimant to the French throne—because he was on too friendly terms with the Empress Eugénie. According to Mr. Harold Kurtz, his father had written in his will, "I leave nothing to Victor. I do not wish him to be present at my funeral."

However, Prince Victor, whom I met frequently

* Born at Meudon, 1862; died at Brussels, 1926.

in London in 1919, was most friendly with the Empress Eugénie and took refuge in England with his wife, the beautiful Princess Clémentine, daughter of Leopold II of Belgium, during the First World War when Belgium was invaded by the German armies.

He came every week to see me, to talk French and to add to his collection of historical French memoirs. When he left England in 1919 to return to Belgium he came to say goodbye and told me that he had had the opportunity of tasting every pleasure and every form of enjoyment, but that the only true and lasting joy he had had was that of his friends the books.

I have often thought about Prince Victor Napoleon's last words to me and realize that what has made me love books is not only the amenities but the sheer delight or ecstasy of life-enhancing book collecting, and I am not the only one who has found his life gladdened by books and literature, as will be seen on the following pages.

M. L. E.
Oxford, 1966

Chapter I

"*Non, non, je ne veux pas être matelot!*" This, my parents used to tell me, was the first sentence that I uttered, at the age of five, when suffering from a stormy crossing in the Channel from Dieppe to New-haven. We were on an old paddle-wheel steamer, which may, for all I know, have been the identical one on which, only a few years ago, I crossed from Lisbon to Barreiro on my way to Seville, via the south of Portugal. To explain why this definite decision was uttered in French I must go back even further in time.

I was born in January 1883, in Paris, where my parents had met, and as my father was engaged in business there, they changed their residence for England only in 1888, when I was five years old. The reason my father moved from France to England was that he had been very successful in promoting a new French invention that he was unable to produce in France but could produce in England.

For many years my father endeavored to find backers in London who were willing to finance new inventions, and I remember some of the inventions with which he was connected. As a rule, however, his interest in them was not rewarded by success. People in England were slow to adopt new ideas.

I remember being taken for a ride in an early motorcar and having one of the earliest phonographs. My father endeavored to obtain the production of the automatic telephone and the first automatic glass-cutting machine. One day, as a schoolboy, I was taken to an office in the City where the first Paulsen wire-recording machine was installed and was amazed to hear the Prince of Wales, later King Edward VII, exclaiming in a very guttural voice, "I am verry bleezed with this woondervol mesheen." This, however, did not diminish my loyalty to the Throne.

Shortly before the First World War my father was negotiating with a professor in Russia who had invented a machine for closed-circuit television to be used in factories for the supervision of workers. I remember tearing up the documents after my father's death. Today I wish I had kept them to be preserved in the South Kensington Science Museum.

As far as I am able to ascertain my family history runs as follows: Shortly after 1531 Judah Oppenheim* and his wife, Edel, left the town of Heidelberg and moved to Frankfort on the Main. Their descendants returned to Heidelberg in 1614 after the expulsion of the Jews from Frankfort. Later, part of the family went back to Frankfort, where the

* In later years the family made use of the adjectival form of the name, *viz.*, Oppenheimer.

oldest house which they owned in the ghetto was called the Red Hart, the same as the house in which, in 1531, they had lived in Heidelberg.

One of those who went back was Wolf Oppenheim of Heidelberg (married to the daughter of Aaron of Mainz), who took up residence in Frankfort in 1670. He married a second time in Frankfort and, in partnership with his new brothers-in-law, dealt in precious stones. This profession was carried on by the Oppenheim family until 1914, when my uncles in Paris (who had continued in the old tradition), gave up their business there.

In 1878, my maternal grandfather, Moses Michel Oppenheimer (who was married in 1843), died, and, in consequence, my mother, his only daughter, left for Paris to rejoin her four stepbrothers. The firm in Paris, at 7 Rue Lepelletier, just off the Boulevard des Italiens, bore the name "Les Fils de H. Marcus Oppenheimer," after my great-great-grandfather Herz Marcus Oppenheimer, born in 1785. It was in Paris that my mother met my father.

In Paris my mother had a number of relatives, including two sisters of her father, who became French by their marriage. The husband of one of them was Monsieur Edmond Rhodé (a cousin), a manufacturer of silk sewing thread; the other, Rosalie, was married to Monsieur Abraham Neuburger. Of her children, the eldest, Gustave, became the director of the Rothschild Frères bank. A second son, Léon, was the head of "French Affairs" in the same bank. He was the husband of Claire Émilie

Weil, whose cousin Jeanne (died 1905) married Dr. Adrien Proust. A daughter, Pauline Neuburger, married Dr. Philip Hauser.

The history of Gustave and Léon Neuburger is intimately connected with that of the house of Rothschild. Dr. Hauser, however, was an unusual man in another sphere of activity. A Hungarian by birth, he studied medicine in Germany at the feet of Max von Pettenkofer, one of the most eminent German medical men, and came to Paris to seek employment. At the time he arrived a terrible outbreak of cholera was decimating Morocco, and the Barons Rothschild, anxious to do something to help the thousands of Moroccan Jews who were without medical assistance or advice, sent the young Dr. Philip Hauser to fight the plague. After superhuman efforts in Morocco and the subsidence of the plague, Dr. Hauser crossed the Straits and settled, as the only civilian doctor, in Gibraltar and then married Pauline Neuburger, my mother's first cousin.

Dr. Hauser, soon after marriage, was able to save Gibraltar from being declared infested by the plague, and, for his good services, the War Office gave him the unusual privilege of allowing his wife to give birth to their children in Gibraltar itself, thus making them British subjects and citizens of Gibraltar. In all other cases the wives of foreigners had to leave that place for the nearest Spanish town or village to give birth to their children. Gibraltar was such a tiny town that there was no room for new citizens.

After some years' medical practice as the only civilian physician, Dr. Hauser decided to seek a wider field for his talent and in 1872 moved to the nearest big Spanish city, Seville, where he was the leading physician for twenty-five years. The town was so appreciative of his services that he was named "Adoptive son of Seville," and a street was named after him. After a quarter of a century Dr. Hauser moved once more, and for the last time, to the Spanish capital, where Queen Maria Christina, mother of Alfonso XIII, had called him as her physician. In December 1920, on my first visit to Madrid, I had the pleasure of making his acquaintance and that of his wife, my cousin Pauline, both splendid figures in their old age.

Dr. Hauser was the author of numerous medical and other works. Among his earlier publications is found *Nouvelles Considérations sur la mortalité de la première enfance en Espagne, comparée avec celle de la France. Mémoire lu au Congrès International d'Hygiène tenu à Paris, 1–10 Août, 1878* (Seville, 1881). Later works included *Seville from the Medical Point of View* and *Les Grecs et les Sémites*.

Dr. Hauser's oldest son, Enrique, took Spanish nationality and in time became Government Inspector of Mines, a member of the Spanish Academy, and a well-known scientist. His younger son, Lionel, born in Gibraltar, in 1868, had a very different career. At the age of four Lionel left Gibraltar for Seville, where he was educated. At the age of fourteen he was sent to Paris and left the École Commerciale in 1886 with the *prix d'honneur* of the Minister of Commerce.

Studying practical commerce in Hamburg and in 1889 in London, he became interested in banking. After leaving the Crédit Lyonnais in London, he received an important post in 1893 at the Barcelona branch of the same bank. In 1899, when the director of the Barcelona branch was appointed director of the St. Petersburg agency, Lionel joined him in Russia. In 1900 the Paris Crédit Lyonnais made him assistant director of a branch in Seville, where he remained until 1903. He then left the Crédit Lyonnais to join the famous bank of M. M. Warburg and Company, of Hamburg, who were agents for the Rothschild Frères bank in Paris and represented the famous New York bank of Kuhn, Loeb and Company.

In 1907 the Banque de Paris et des Pays Bas and Kuhn, Loeb and Company, of New York, decided to start a Franco-American bank in Paris, and Lionel Hauser was selected as one of the directors, with the special task of representing the interests of the American bank. In the meantime, there was a crisis in New York, and the founding of the bank was postponed and eventually abandoned. In view of this, Lionel Hauser was asked to remain in Paris to represent the two banks of Warburg and Kuhn, Loeb, and there he undertook the floating of a number of loans for some of the most important American railways, to the tune of many hundred million dollars.

In 1914 the war put an end to his representation of the Warburg bank, but he continued to represent the New York bank of Kuhn, Loeb; and, through connections with Mr. C. S. Gulbenkian, he introduced on the New York market shares of the Royal Dutch, the Shell, and the Transport Trading companies. In 1924 he became a naturalized Frenchman.

Lionel Hauser was the most unpretentious and modest of men, in spite of, or perhaps because of, his high standards and great knowledge.

When the close of the Second World War made it possible to communicate from England with France again, I immediately wrote to his last address in Paris. The letter was forwarded and he wrote me a very short account of what had happened to him and his wife during the German occupation. All his property, clothing, furniture, et cetera, had been stolen from him, and in reply to my request as to what he would like me to send him (I thought he would be in dire straits), he replied that all he wanted was a pot of Keiller's Dundee Marmalade!

Lionel Hauser met the Proust family when he first came to Paris, being introduced by his uncle Gustave Neuburger to Marcel Proust's mother, whose cousin, née Claire Émilie Weil, was Lionel Hauser's aunt by marriage to Léon Neuburger. Madame Adrien Proust wished Lionel Hauser to become a friend of her son Marcel, hoping that he would prove to be a good influence on him. However, as Lionel Hauser was for years occupied by his studies and later was absent from Paris, there was little or no communication between the two. Later, when Lionel Hauser returned to France, their relations became much closer.

Dr. Adrien Proust had an account at the Rothschild bank, and, when his parents died, Marcel Proust found himself heir to a small fortune, the income of which would have allowed him to await carefree the hour of his celebrity.

Unfortunately for Proust, there were among his numerous friends some young people who were frequenters of the Paris Stock Exchange and every now and then gave him tips which were supposed to help him to increase his fortune. Foolishly he believed them and started to speculate. As the stocks and shares which he had inherited were deposited at the Rothschild bank, his orders to sell passed through the hands of M. Léon Neuburger, who was in despair at seeing Marcel Proust selling sound shares which his parents had accumulated and replacing them by very doubtful and speculative paper.

Léon Neuburger, in order to put a stop to the dilapidation of Marcel Proust's fortune, suggested to the latter that he should entrust his friend Lionel Hauser with the management of his affairs, and Proust at once accepted. In this way Lionel Hauser became Proust's private banker, and during the course of years they exchanged some 365 letters. When Lionel Hauser was in his late eighties he wrote to me at Oxford about these letters and, through me, sold them to the Library of the University of Illinois.

The collection then sold includes some 195 of Proust's autograph letters and about 170 of Lionel Hauser's letters in carbon copies. Proust's letters alone are well over one thousand pages, some single letters consisting of no less than sixteen pages. Their interest is considerable, because they show an aspect of Proust's character that is little known and they are of great variety, treating many subjects besides financial matters. At the time of their sale to the University of Illinois, permission for their publication had not yet been given by Proust's niece. Madame Mante-Proust.

Recently, however, Professor Philip Kolb, of the Department of French of the University of Illinois, has obtained Madame Mante-Proust's authorization to publish Proust's correspondence with Lionel Hauser in a small noncommercial edition by the University of Illinois Press.

At a later date Proust's letters will be reissued in Professor Kolb's edition of Proust's *Correspondance générale,* which was authorized some years ago and on which Professor Kolb is still working for publication under contract with the Librairie Plon, of Paris. It was the authorization for a separate volume of this Proust-Hauser correspondence which Madame Mante-Proust had been reluctant to give, and which Professor Kolb has now obtained.*

Another Neuburger daughter, Louise, was married

* As Lionel Hauser's letters too are interesting, Professor Kolb hopes to give many of them for publication along with those of Proust.

to the famous French philosopher Henri Bergson and outlived him, dying shortly after the Second World War. Their only child, a daughter, Jeanne, born in 1893, became a famous sculptress and artist and died in 1961.

In March 1963 an "In Memoriam" exhibition of her drawings and engravings took place in the Galerie Bernheim-Jeune, Paris. The illustrated catalogue issued at the time shows that she was a favorite pupil of Antoine Bourdelle and that Édouard Herriot admired her work.

I first met the world of print when a baby. My father used to bribe me daily to brave the terrors of an ancient form of cold shower which was fixed outside his bedroom. Prettily colored broadsides were handed to me after I had manfully undergone the breathtaking experience of the cold shower and returned to my warm bed. These popular cartoons, called *Images d'Épinal,* were still current in the 1880's and consisted of a number of small highly colored pictures with a few lines of French text under each describing the adventures of Cinderella, Tom Thumb, Little Red Ridinghood, Sleeping Beauty and other fairy-tale characters.

My next literary remembrance is that of Victor Hugo's lying-in-state. Four months after an immense state banquet to celebrate his eighty-third birthday, Victor Hugo died, on the night of May 31, 1885. His remains lay in state for twenty-four hours on top of a mammoth urn which filled the Arc de Triomphe.

At the end of the Champs Élysées mounted cuirassiers in their picturesque uniform with bright breastplates and gleaming helmets with horse-tail pendants stood guard in a wide circle while funeral pyres blazed all around.

"The Arc de Triomphe was opened for the first time for the return of Napoleon's ashes from St. Helena. In 1885 the Arc de Triomphe was opened for the second time when the body of Victor Hugo lay in state at the foot of the monument for the entire night before it was transported to the Panthéon. On this occasion the Parisians witnessed the most gigantic procession that has ever filed through the streets of Paris. Of the 800,000 mourners, most had never read the works of the great poet, but they revered him as a defender of democratic freedom and above all as a writer who had been courageous enough to expose the sufferings of the poor. The Guard of Honour round the coffin was mounted by twelve young French poets."*

* Eric Whelpton, *Paris Cavalcade* (1959).

Chapter II

On their arrival in England my parents settled in Hove, at 33 Wilbury Road (from the upper stories of the house one could watch county cricket being played), where I was placed in charge of the customary governesses who taught me to recite poetry and to read. Later I went to a Dame's School in the next road, where, because of my French accent, I earned the nickname "Froggy."

About this time my parents added to my bookcase the two volumes of *Alice, Chatterbox* and, to my great delight, the current volumes of the *Boy's Own Paper*. In those days the *Boy's Own Paper* published stories by Talbot Baines Reed, Jules Verne, and other excellent authors, so that my interest was aroused, and by a lucky chance my parents were able to buy the complete set for me. Unfortunately the *Alices* were not first editions, and the set of the *Boy's Own Paper* has also long ago disappeared.

I regret today the loss of the first editions of Henty which have become so fashionable again, the early editions of Struwwelpeter, and the decorative children's books by Kate Greenaway, such as *An Apple Pie* and *Under the Window*.

When I was nine the household moved to London, near Colet Court and St. Paul's School, and very soon I was interested in the neighboring bookshops, though my collecting in those days was eminently practical; editions of the Latin and Greek classics, dictionaries, et cetera, were looked for in the book-stalls outside the Pro-Cathedral near Holland Park, at Cooper's in Hammersmith, and later on the push-carts in the Farringdon Road.

Life at St. Paul's, then under the guidance of the famous High Master Frederick William Walker, or the Old Man as all the boys called him, was strenu-ous and has been excellently described by Mr. Hubert Arthur Sams in his privately printed *Pauline and Old Pauline, 1884–1931*. Like Mr. Sams, I began London school life at Colet Court or "Bewsher's," al-though I entered it only after Mr. Sams had left. The Preparatory School belonged to "Sammy," or Mr. Samuel Bewsher, the bursar of St. Paul's School, and he placed his brother Jimmy Bewsher as head-master and his sister as a teacher of the youngest children.

In my time, at St. Paul's, which has been so well described in Volume I of Sir Montague Compton Mackenzie's *Sinister Street,* there was only one bibliophile among the masters to my knowledge, and that was the Rev. Horace Elam (now depicted as Mr. Olim, in Raymond's delightful novel *Mr. Olim*), although there were other masters who had a love of books, such as Mr. T. R. Holmes, the author of *Caesar in Gaul.*

Elam was the most unusual of our teachers, and he apparently terrified Mr. Sams, who did not understand his jokes and his sense of humor. He was very fond of the cane and indulged in it to such an extent that while I was in his class he was forbidden the further use of it. He was eccentric in every way and liked to display his eccentricity in school. I thought him the only really likable educator, with an excellent knowledge of French, and I delighted in the extraordinary anecdotes he used to tell us.

Mr. Elam was afraid of no one, not even of Dr. Walker, the terrifying High Master, whose brusque and rude manner and booming voice made him most unpopular among the parents of the boys at school. He hated the mothers coming to see him and generally ended interviews with them by asking them to take their boys away. He was interested only in pupils who specialized in Latin and Greek literature, and he despised all other forms of education. There was a feud between the High Master and Mr. Elam, but as both were masters of the art of rudeness they respected each other for their toughness.

Mr. Elam was not satisfied to cram our heads with Latin and Greek grammar, but was interested in educating us, not so much by his own example as by the way in which he was able to illustrate the history of the Greeks and Romans.

He had a prodigious memory, and in his days at Oxford he is supposed to have carried all the university prizes before him, but owing to lack of social influence, instead of becoming a powerful bishop or archbishop, he had to take refuge from unemployment as what he called a "low-caste downtrodden badly paid usher" in a school which he regarded as merely a hothouse for producing boys who would carry off scholarships for the universities. This was entirely against his way of thinking. He was against snobbery of all kinds.

I remember him once examining me and on eliciting that my parents were of German origin and had met in Paris, where I was born, and that I was a Jew, he said: "Well, that shows you are a mongrel, but after all mongrels are the best dogs to have."

Year after year, as the contents of his classes changed, he would repeat the same stories. For instance, he would describe how Mr. and Mrs. Smythe (not Smith, of course) would put on evening dress every evening in their two-room flat, where they would be served by a kitchen maid who also dressed specially for dinner. The first course consisted of soup made from Liebig's extract of beef and tepid water, and this was followed by a large dish with a shining cover which was brought in and put before Mr. Smythe; the cover having been taken off with a flourish, two small red herrings became visible, Mr. Smythe thereupon said, "My dear, may I help you to a little fish?" "Yes, my dear," said Mrs. Smythe. The fish course having been removed, another dish was brought in with three minute sausages ("bags of mystery," Mr. Elam used to call them). The same rigmarole continued, and Mr. Smythe very carefully gave Mrs. Smythe a helping of the sausages. The dessert course consisted of half a dozen stewed prunes, which were shared out in equal portions, and this was followed by cups of coffee. After a while, Mrs. Smythe retired to the withdrawing room; Mr. Smythe donned a smoking cap and rejoined Mrs. Smythe only after having smoked a twopenny cigar!

I am sorry I have forgotten many of the anecdotes, which were meant to teach us a sensible way of life and a condemnation of rank snobbery, so prevalent among the middle classes in the nineties. But I shall never forget his announcing that he was saving from his "miserable pittance as an usher enough to buy a farthing rushlight to guide him to the workhouse in his retirement."

He habitually wore clothes that had become so shiny that one could almost use them as a looking glass, and he forbade us ever to recognize him or take off our caps to him outside the school premises. He told us that once when he was on board a Channel steamer he had seen a boy wearing the school cap, whereupon he hid in the stokehold till the boat arrived at Dover, for fear of being noticed by the boy.

Although he was popularly supposed to have an enormous number of books, no boy was ever invited to his house; outside school hours and in the Hammersmith Road, he could be seen fleeing from the sight of anybody wearing the school cap. As a matter of fact, Horace Elam had a remarkable and very large collection of books, as was shown when his library was sold during the First World War at Hodgson's Auction Rooms in Chancery Lane. He was a great expert on Spain, and he revised Murray's famous guidebook on Spain, which was first written by Richard Ford.

As a postscript to these few lines about an unforgettable education, I would like to add the following anecdote. In November 1918 the revolt of the German Army enabled me, an internee, to get out of the Ruhleben camp for enemy civilians and make the necessary arrangements to escape from Germany, which had held me captive for four years, and to go to Switzerland, where my parents were staying for my father's health. Soon after I arrived in Switzerland I got in touch with the British Legation in Berne and was asked to contact a special department to prove my identity. There I was joined by a friend from Ruhleben, Maxwell Wimpole, a barrister, who had been of great service to all the civilian prisoners in the prison camp. I was interviewed by a middle-aged temporary Foreign Office functionary. On hearing that I had been to St. Paul's, he immediately cried out: "And what did you think of Elam? Did you know him?" The stories I was able to exchange with my examiner were the best proof of my identity.

If my readers wish to hear more about Mr. Elam, who remains firmly in the memory of all who knew him, I can only refer him again to Ernest Raymond's *Mr. Olim* and to Sir Montague Compton Mackenzie's recently published *Octave Two*.

On sixpence a week pocket money (which was the normal allowance schoolboys had) it was not easy to buy many books, but those were indeed fortunate days for the lover of English literature; at Barker's, at Pontings', and at Derry & Toms's in High Street, Kensington, practically all the works of Dickens, Thackeray, Captain Marryat, Lever, et cetera, were obtainable for 9¾d a volume, each in legible type and well bound in brown and green cloth. Thus, most boys were able to start small libraries of their own.

At St. Paul's there were two good libraries. One was a boys' library full of Henty, Captain Marryat and other excellent works of fiction which could be borrowed daily and taken home; the other was the principal school library, which was open only to members of the upper forms and contained, in addition to the most useful texts and scholarly books, first editions of Milton, who had formerly attended the school.

Among my fellow pupils at St. Paul's was Rupert Beswicke Howorth. He was three years older than myself and the second son of Sir Henry H. Howorth, a member of the Royal Society and famous as the author of a standard and unsurpassed history of the Mongols. After leaving St. Paul's, Howorth entered the British Civil Service, first on the Board of Education and then with the Treasury. He was transferred in 1930 to the Office of the Cabinet, where he remained as Deputy Secretary to the

Cabinet to 1942. From 1938 to 1942 he was also Clerk of the Privy Council.

There was also P.T.B. "Tubby" Clayton, two years younger than myself. At Oxford he passed the final theological examination with First Class Honours and was appointed Curate of Portsea, where he remained from 1910 to 1914. Appointed temporary chaplain to the armed forces (he later became brigade chaplain), in 1915 he opened Talbot House (named after Gilbert Talbot, a son of the Bishop of Winchester) at Poperinghe, in the Ypres salient. In 1920 he refounded Talbot House as Toc H—a movement to teach the younger generation class reconciliation and unselfish service. He has toured the world on behalf of this movement. He was Chaplain to King George VI and since 1952 has been Chaplain to the Queen. He has written much on current social and religious affairs.

I also remember such figures as Sir Compton Mackenzie, Richard Jennings, the distinguished bibliophile (he has given his name to the phrase "Jennings condition," which indicates the perfect condition of a book and its binding), R. H. Wilenski, the art historian, and many others who unfortunately are no longer with us.

I remember Clayton and myself going home from school along the Edith Road and being roughly handled by some Fulham toughs; our respective mothers arranged to wait in hiding and waylay our attackers, who fled after having had the worst of it.

I still remember the small bottles of eucalyptus oil being presented to my father by Clayton's father (R. B. B. Clayton, J.P.), who was introducing it from Queensland. In those days a lump of sugar with a few drops of eucalyptus oil was supposed to be an unfailing remedy for influenza.

In my last year at school I spent an enjoyable time in the History Eighth which was founded and guided by Robert Francis Cholmeley (1862–1947), who later in 1909 became Headmaster of Owen's School, Islington.

One of the masters who made a most vivid impression on me was Digby LaMotte (of Trinity College, Oxford), who was always beautifully dressed and who in addition to being a good classical scholar and Master of the "Seventh" was an excellent French master. One of our duties in the "Seventh" class was to provide him with gardenia buttonholes, which he accepted with condescension. As a grandson of a peer (Lord Digby) he felt he had to show his aristocratic descent both in action and diction. At one time the Rev. Horace Elam spoke of him, as he did of most of the other masters, with contempt, but from one day to another they became almost bosom friends and it was a strange sight to see the dandified exceedingly tall and well-dressed LaMotte, a gardenia in his buttonhole, walking side by side in eager conversation with the shabbily dressed, sardonic Elam.

Although I obtained a History Exhibition on leaving St. Paul's, my parents did not wish me to go up to a university, as they thought I was too young.

Chapter III

As a boy I always had an inclination to become a publisher, although the art of publishing books was a complete mystery to me. I was accordingly sent in 1901 through a friend of my father's to Mr. C. G. Luzac (descendant of the famous Dutch Huguenot Etienne Luzac), an Oriental publisher and bookseller, at 46 Great Russell Street, opposite the British Museum, where his successors still carry on business.

At that time my father was one of the directors of the *Sunday Special,* a rival of the *Sunday Times,* and a fellow director of J. T. Grein, the founder of the Independent Theatre and consul for the Congo. Mr. C. G. Luzac was a friend of J. T. Grein, both being members of the famous Dutch Club in Piccadilly. The *Sunday Special,* owing to Grein's interest in the theatre, promoted special Sunday matinees of plays that could not then be staged commercially and gave away the seats to their readers. I remember in this way attending early performances of Bernard Shaw's *Arms and the Man, Candida, You Never Can Tell,* and *The Man of Destiny,* and some of Ibsen's plays.

At Mr. Luzac's shop (he was then without a part-

ner), for the first time hundreds of books and manuscripts in all languages and of all epochs surrounded
me, and I was left to catalogue them as well as I
could. A lack of knowledge of Arabic, Chinese and
Indian scripts soon showed me how great were the
drawbacks of an almost exclusively classical education, and after a year's work in Luzac's shop, in
October 1902 I went up to Queen's College, Oxford,
to get a knowledge of Sanskrit and to make at least
some acquaintance with Arabic, Chinese and other
Oriental scripts and literatures. In 1902 Queen's
was lucky enough to possess Professor Sayce and
Grenfell and Hunt as fellows, and the provost was
very kind in allowing me to plod along in my own
way, leaving all the usual subjects and examinations
to one side and devoting most of my time to Sanskrit
and Arabic.

Instead of preparing for the two important examinations in classics (Latin, Greek, philosophy and
history), I was able to spend the whole time in
studying Sanskrit with Professor A. A. Macdonell
(Boden Professor of Sanskrit), where I was one of
four or five students only, and in private coaching
in Arabic with Professor Thatcher, of Manchester
College, who subsequently left Oxford for one of the
Dominions and was later the author of a standard
Arabic grammar.

As India was still administered by Englishmen,
there were a number of lectures on Oriental subjects
which were of special interest to me, in view of the
profession for which I was preparing. At the Indian

Institute, an important building paid for by wealthy Indian maharajahs, lectures were given on the Laws of Manu (primitive Indian Law) and on many of the languages of India. I was unable to find any time for the Chinese language as I had hoped, but was able to read much about Chinese literature.

The Union Society (the club to which both senior and junior members of the university belonged) had an extensive library, including both English and French fiction. This helped me to keep up my general knowledge of literature.

In the afternoons (at least after I had been fortunate enough to win my scholarship), I used to go with friends to the River Thames and profit by the loan of one of the flat-bottomed boats, or "punts," which are peculiar to Oxford. These were freely at the disposal of the members of Queen's College at Queen's College Boat House, at the bottom of Christ Church Meadows. We used to find our way slowly up the River Cherwell, discussing whatever subject was nearest our hearts.

Those were the days of private breakfasts and lunch parties in one's rooms in College; the custom of taking all meals in the College Hall only began with the Second World War. I remember one tea party to which I had invited an assortment of my friends—my best friend, a Methodist mathematician who used to drive out on Sundays in a dogcart to outlying parishes to preach and conduct services in outlying villages where there was no resident minister; a young Jesuit who was a resident at Pope's Hall and an eminent mathematician; a Japanese; and an Indian fellow student—bringing together every variety of earnest religious thought.

The contrast between those days of comparative leisure and today in Oxford is tremendous. In term-time the City of Oxford existed only for the students, who numbered a very few thousand. When the students were on vacation (six months in the year) the City was dead, and during the long vacation in summer many shops shut altogether, tourists were unknown and "summer schools" were unheard of, while today the crowds on the Oxford pavements are so great that it is difficult to avoid being hustled off them into the line of teeming automobile traffic.

Blackwell's bookshop in Broad Street was then a veritable treasure trove of rare and unusual books. It was not too difficult to start a collection of Chinese and other Oriental books, as there were very few competitors in Oxford.

Some of my friends used to come from London to spend the day at Blackwell's, looking for old and rare books, which they could pick up for the proverbial song. This famous shop, celebrated in poetry and prose, was then ruled by Sir Basil Blackwell's father and was famous for its large well-supplied antiquarian department. There were then only a few bookseller's assistants employed; today there are three or four hundred, and Blackwell's has extended into publishing, printing and bookbinding, with music, paperback, stationery and children's book shops.

After a year's work at Oxford, during which time I was lucky in picking up a University Boden Sanskrit Scholarship, in April 1903 I was invited by Professor Sylvain Lévi to continue my studies at the Sorbonne, in Paris, and there for the first time I was able to indulge in real book collecting. In the autumn of 1903 the bookstalls on the quays were full of interesting books and not filled with the rubbishy remainders and fake prints which they display today. Then the *bouquinistes* were the owners of their stocks of books and eagerly replenished their stalls; today they are nearly all employees of larger bookshops who use the quays to dispose of their overstock. For a franc in 1903 it was possible to pick up on the same stall in two successive weeks a copy of *Götz von Berlichingen* (which was privately printed for Goethe as a young man and is one of the rarest books in German literature) and a first edition of Heine's *Buch der Lieder*.

In the offices of Ernest Leroux, the chief Orientalist publisher in France, there remained bundles of books unsold at auction sales of famous Oriental libraries which had taken place under his auspices some thirty or forty years before. It was indeed pleasant to yield to temptation and buy, at bargain prices, French books on Buddhism and other Oriental religions and precious early Chinese printed books. Although the contents of the Chinese classics and novels I then bought remained a sealed book to me, I was able, by means of Mayer's Chinese Reader's Manual and Wylie's indispensable book on Chinese literature, to catalogue what became, after some months, a considerable Chinese library.

Whilst pursuing my studies at the École des Hautes Études in the Sorbonne I also heard lectures at the Collège de France, where I naturally attended the courses held by Professor Sylvain Lévi and in addition, for my own satisfaction, the last lectures given by Professor Jules Oppert, who explained to a very small audience of three hearers the newly discovered Laws of Hammurabi. He was very nearly blind, but he was able to quote the German and French Law Codes by heart. The other two men to whom he lectured have both left us. One, Charles Fossey, succeeded Oppert as professor of Assyriology; although he died very young he left an excellent standard book on Assyrian magic, which appeared in 1902. The other, Professor Nahum Schlouzsch, emigrated to Israel after making lengthy voyages through Africa, visiting little-known Jewish communities; he died a few years ago at an advanced age.

After spending some twelve months in Paris in the Latin Quarter, working on my thesis and being spoiled in my leisure hours by my mother's two bachelor stepbrothers, I returned to London to work in the Oriental Students' Room at the British Museum, then under the guardianship of Dr. Lionel Barnett; the keeper of Oriental books was still Professor Robert Kennaway Douglas, the expert in Chinese and author of the greatest Chinese dictionary.

In those days it was a delight to spend one's spare time in old Paternoster Row (long since destroyed by Nazi bombs) and pick up for a few pence Chinese books containing impressions of ancient seals in the so-called tadpole character. With luck it was also possible to find those rare specimens of Chinese works where text and illustrations were printed white on black, reversing the usual order of things. These books were subsequently purchased by Professor Douglas for the British Museum's department of Oriental books and manuscripts. I was still working at my thesis when the question arose as to my future.

While at Luzac's I was shown one day a manuscript which had been bought, before my arrival there, as an Oriental manuscript. It was triangular in form, on vellum, and written in strange characters. It bore a Latin title in rather strange dog Latin, announcing that the Comte de Saint-Germain had traveled throughout the world. I was very puzzled by this, and took it home and broke the cipher by means of the tetragrammaton. The manuscript, when deciphered, turned out to be much the usual compilation of magical practices, written in French, on how to find hidden treasures, formulae to procure the appearance of helpful spirits, such as are to be found in the numerous versions of *Le Dragon Rouge*. The manuscript was dated and obviously had been used by the very mysterious Comte de Saint-Germain, about whom so much has been written but of whom so little is known. Eventually the manuscript was purchased and joined the remarkable collection of old alchemical tracts and manuscripts of my cousin Lionel Hauser in Paris.

On my leaving Luzac's in 1902 for Oxford my father had been informed by my employer that on my return from the university he would be willing to accept me as a junior partner. However, after I had been in Paris a few months, Luzac was stricken by an attack of meningitis and died. His widow offered the firm to my father for the sum of five hundred pounds, but my father, because I was under age and without business experience, considered it unwise to buy the firm. He was impressed also by the fact that after Luzac had spent half a lifetime in publishing Oriental books the business was being offered for such a small sum. He therefore thought it best for me not to continue to specialize in Orientalia but to learn more about the general book trade and especially to get some knowledge of early European manuscripts and early printed books.

I had left Luzac's when, in January 1905, I made the acquaintance of C. Poma, a former Italian Consul in China. Signor Poma, who had resided for three years in northern China, had used his leisure time to form a Manchu collection, in order to preserve some of the monuments of the Manchu tongue, which was then practically as extinct as Latin, and its use having been very restricted, its monuments, books and documents were already very scarce.

The Consul was living at Biella, Italy, and offered the collection of sixty-four items for sale. It included eighteen books, two wooden tablets, and six

Manchu-Chinese Diplomas of the Emperor T'ung Chih, who acceded to the throne in 1862 and died in 1875. In addition there was a remarkable collection of silk scrolls, each several yards long, rolled up and covered with a fine fabric of dark red, containing a Chinese and a Manchu text bestowing a title on some worthy official or on his deserving parents. The two texts ran, with beautifully designed characters and letters of different colors, on many sections of different silk, whose color differed from one another and from the superimposed text, so that the effect was one of great beauty and variety.

Two samples of such diplomas were described in the review *Toung-Pao* (Leiden, 1897, Volume 8), and their contents were analyzed by Père Hoang, in his *Mélanges sur l'administration* (Shanghai, 1902).

It was difficult for Signor Poma to obtain diplomas of this kind, as "Degradation was the penalty for a Mandarin mortgaging for money a diploma of decoration." Only the tragic events of 1900 made it possible for Signor Poma, with great difficulty, to form a series of twenty-nine diplomas ranging from 1736 to the date I acquired the collection.

In addition to the above-mentioned manuscripts there were two very interesting amulets and various rubbings of Manchu inscriptions from the Imperial palaces and Buddhist temples.

Chapter IV

An opportunity now arose to secure a position in a
firm at Munich. This firm, specially devoted to illuminated and early manuscripts and rare books, had
been founded about 1858 by the senior partner
Ludwig Rosenthal, who was still alive and flourish-
ing when I joined the company in 1905. This remarkable man might be termed the founder of the
modern school of bookselling. Born in 1840, in the
little Bavarian village of Feldheim, he had walked
many miles daily to a larger village to obtain in-
struction in Latin and literature.

Ludwig was acquainted with most of the famous
collectors in Europe and the United States, and in
the course of his dealings with missals, breviaries and
other rare liturgical books, he had acquired an
astonishing knowledge of early printed books. At
one time he had specialized in Catholic theology and
had supplied many European monasteries. Once at
a local fair in Munich he had been fortunate enough
to pick up two halves of a small tarnished copper
globe on which were depicted two hemispheres. One
of the two halves bore the maker's name Robert de
Bailly and the date 1530, which led to the conjecture

that the place of manufacture was probably Dieppe. Herr Rosenthal bought them, took them to his home and thoroughly cleaned them and pieced them together. He was able to show, after considerable research, that the two hemispheres comprised one of the oldest metal globes, showing the discoveries of Giovanni da Verrazano in the New World.

The globe contains the Equator, the Tropics and the Polar Circles. America, bearing the name "America" and "Mundus Novus," is divided into four parts—North, Central, South America and the Archipelago—and on it appear the following names: Terra Laboratoris (Labrador), Bachaliaio (*bacalhao* is the Portuguese word for codfish), Parias, Tanacnoi, et cetera. The continent lying opposite the southernmost point of America is called Brasielie Regio.

The most interesting characteristic of the globe is the fact that the results of Verrazano's travels are marked by "Terra Verrazana"; except on the maps of Girolamo Verrazano (Giovanni's brother) of 1529, the name is nowhere to be found. It must not be forgotten that in April 1524 the Italian navigator explored the New York Bay area, hence the naming of the new Verrazano Bridge in New York.

This priceless globe (dated 1530 in two places) is the earliest to show Verrazano's discoveries. Earlier cartographic mention of these early discoveries is to be found only on Vesconto di Maggiolo's map (1527) and that of the above-named Girolamo.

The label used in displaying the globe in the

Pierpont Morgan Library reads as follows: "This is one of the finest Globes of the period. It is signed and dated by its maker. It is turned so the Western Hemisphere faces the center of the room. The Atlantic coast is shown with considerable accuracy, especially that of Central and South America, and records the results of the explorations of Giovanni da Verrazano for Francis I in 1524. The Pacific Coast of North America is fanciful—it is labeled 'Incognita'—and reflects Verrazano's conception of a large gulf penetrating the continent. The continent is inscribed 'Verrazana.' Also shown is the Northwest Passage to the Pacific Ocean."

On another occasion Ludwig Rosenthal discovered an unknown "Fifth Book" of François Rabelais. It was a very small book of sixty-four leaves, still in its original sixteenth-century binding of calf leather gilt, with fleur-de-lys and blind tooling. The binding led one to the belief that it was probably bound at Lyons, and while it did not bear the name of the printer or the place of printing, it was probably also printed at Lyons. The book bore the title *Le Cinquième Livre des faictz et dictz du noble Pantagruel. Auquelz sont compris les grans Abus & d'esordonée vie de, Plusieurs Estatz, de ce monde. Composez par m. Francoys Rabelays D'octeur en Mendecine & Abstracteur de quinte Essence. Imprimé en Lan Mil cinq cens Quarante neuf (1549).* But it was certainly not written by Rabelais and must be called a pseudo-Rabelaisian Book Five, in spite of the fact that it was printed during Rabelais's lifetime. The so-called "official" Book Five of Rabelais is posthumous, having been published for the first time in 1564, and is generally considered to be equally apocryphal.

Inside the cover of the book was a manuscript note asserting the fact that an unknown C. Mellinger purchased the book in Paris in 1549, the very year it was printed.

The discovery of this little book raised enormous interest in France, and the attribution to Rabelais on the title page was bitterly disputed. The controversy was dealt with at length in the first volume of Abel Lefranc's *Revue des études Rabelaisiennes*, pages 29–54 and 122–142. Full details of the book are to be found on page 247 of Plan's Bibliography of Rabelais.

In spite of all research Ludwig Rosenthal's discovery has remained unique. Owing to the controversy about its authorship the book remained for many years unsold in the possession of the firm of Ludwig Rosenthal, and it was only after December 1909 that it was sold and joined the famous library of the late Charles W. Clark. Later, together with Mr. Clark's magnificent collection of Continental first editions, it came into the hands of Dr. A. S. W. Rosenbach for disposal.

In the huge Ludwig Rosenthal warehouse there were about one million volumes, chiefly the result of enormous purchases many years before I arrived in

Munich. The warehouse was a large building, but still there was no longer room enough to permit the books to be stood up on their edges in the usual way of shelving books, and so they were piled up on their sides, in stacks.

One day, as I was going through the stacks, I discovered that some thirty incunabula and early sixteenth-century books chiefly of medical interest were all bound in the same kind of oak board covered with stamped leather. On examining them carefully I found that each of the volumes bore the words "Nicolaus Pol Doctor 1494" in manuscript, on the inside of the front cover. There were quite a number of these books, and when Dr. Edward Clark Streeter, the famous Boston collector of medical books, came to Munich in 1907 he was delighted to buy them all for $800. In 1926, on a visit to Boston, I was fortunate enough to buy the whole series back from him for $5,000, and they were sent to England. There I was able to add a few more important Pol books and issued a *Catalogue of Medical Works from the library of Dr. Nicolaus Pol.*

The collection again found a home in the United States, and a bibliographical monograph, *Nicolaus Pol Doctor 1494,* was published in 1947 in New York by Max H. Fisch. This contains catalogues of the books in the collections now in the Cleveland Medical Association Library and at Yale, and an "inclusive list of books and manuscripts known to have belonged to Nicolaus Pol (467 items)."

Dr. Nicolaus Pol was a distinguished physician in

his day, the court doctor of Holy Roman Emperor Maximilian I, himself a lover and creator of fine books such as the famous *Theuerdanck,* of which copies on vellum and on paper fetch very high prices. In addition to the Pol volumes which came from Munich, the largest surviving collection is in San Candido in the Italian Tirol.

During my stay in Munich, Marion H. Spielman, editor of *The Journal of Art,* and author of many books on art, wished to write a monograph on the authenticity of the known portraits of Shakespeare. After he had bought all the portraits in Ludwig Rosenthal's stock in Munich, most of which seemed to me of small interest, being seemingly copied from each other, we placed an advertisement in the various book-trade papers asking for portraits of Shakespeare. In due course, on a halfpenny "book-report card," a Neapolitan bookseller offered us a portrait of Shakespeare by William Marshall for 250 lire, adding in parenthesis "The portrait is still in the book of poems of Shakespeare, 1640." This seemed much too good to be true, but it was deemed inadvisable to send a telegram. Another halfpenny "book-order form" was used to order the portrait, and within a week the postman brought a small registered package which on being opened disclosed an exceptionally large and fine copy of Shakespeare's poems (London, 1640), in the original calf binding. This was sent for sale to Sotheby's and duly bought (I think by Pickering) for £400. Today this would probably bring £3,000, perhaps more.

Not many old English books appeared on the Continent, where English literature was represented chiefly by French or German reprints of the early nineteenth century, especially those put out by Baudry in Paris. One such book was an edition of Byron which was printed for Galignani and contains the famous reproduction of the autograph letter that has trapped so many collectors.

Many famous bibliophiles came to Ludwig Rosenthal to buy books. Among them were Count Orlov, Count Bobrinsky, Seulesco, Protopopov, and other bibliophiles from Russia, Rumania and Poland who visited Vienna as a second Paris and then went on to Munich before returning home.

One day we received, through my father in London, the offer of a collection of English plays in many volumes. One of the younger Rosenthals, whose turn it was to travel outside Bavaria, went to Norfolk and bought the books of the Francis Longe library, Spixworth, after a somewhat superficial examination. There were something like 1,200 plays bound up into 150 volumes for a member of the Paston family. Among the more unusual and interesting plays found was a first edition of *Fair Em,* also an early *Interlude of Wine Ale and Tobacco contending for superiority*. But what was my surprise after examining the contents of the bound volumes one by one, to find a large and almost unique copy of Milton's *Comus*. This fetched £1,000 at auction at Sotheby's.

At that time most incunabula and early printed books were still to be found in their original bindings, which, when inspected carefully, would occasionally produce fifteenth-century woodcut playing cards in perfect condition, still uncut in sets as they came from the printer, and on occasion fifteenth-century engravings by the monogrammist E.S. were discovered.

In those blissful days of peace it was possible to buy in every market, and I remember the astonishment with which I was greeted by my employers when, after sending a very modest bid for an item in London at Hodgson's "last sale of the season," I was able to produce several prompt copies of Shakespeare's plays bearing most interesting manuscript directions, names of actors, and instructions as to music, et cetera, which had been taken from the Fourth Folio and used in Dublin at a theater for the production of these plays. These prompt copies, which also included some manuscript "parts," were bought by Mr. Henry Clay Folger (1857–1930) and are now among the treasures of the Folger Shakespeare Library in Washington, D.C., together with a copy of the Fourth Folio censored by the Spanish Inquisition.

Mr. Folger's library of Shakespeareana comprised some 70,000 volumes, and was considered to be one of the finest in the United States, if not in the world. It was bequeathed by him to the American nation as the Folger Shakespeare Memorial Library and was installed in a building of its own east of the

Congressional Library in Washington. Mr. Folger, born in New York City, graduated at Amherst at the age of twenty-two and then pursued his studies at the Columbia Law School, New York. He was associated with the Standard Oil Company of New Jersey from 1879 to 1911, when he joined the Standard Oil Company of New York, serving first as president and then as chairman of the board. As a capitalist he was able to secure all the books and Shakespearean relics he desired and will remain forever known as the original founder of the library which bears his name. Today, under wise management, the Folger Library is devoted not only to Shakespeare but also to early English literature of all kinds and to books which illustrate the history of England and English authors before 1800. Mr. Folger left the administration of the Library in the hands of the trustees of Amherst College.

During my stay in Munich I engaged in some journalistic activities and had the great pleasure of inviting Mr. and Mrs. George Bernard Shaw to lunch at my home and afterward taking them to the new zoo just outside Munich. Bernard Shaw was at his spriteliest, full of witticisms. He criticized rather sharply his Austrian translator, Trebitsch, whom, he said, "I keep on as he is an excellent business man." He visited a performance of his *You Never Can Tell* at the Residenz Theater and was amused to find that when one of the actors exclaimed, "But I really must draw the line somewhere," the actor got up and drew the curtains!

Shaw most readily signed his name in my Visitor's Book. He wrote his name in the middle of a blank page, surrounding it with lines so that his name stood out as the middle of the sun with rays extending in all directions. He left no room for his wife to sign, but she wittily added her "Charlotte Shaw" across one of the rays at the bottom of the page.

For some years before 1914 I traveled regularly for the Rosenthal firm in Paris and England. Through Mr. Alfred W. Pollard, of the British Museum, I was introduced to Mr. C. W. Dyson Perrins (1864–1958), of Davenham, Malvern, whom I visited annually thereafter. I was able to sell him some of his finest woodcut books and some of the most unusual of his precious illuminated manuscripts. Three sales realized £888,370.

Chapter V

I returned from a business trip to England on the thirtieth of June 1914, but on the advice of the British consul I did not at once leave, as he promised me that all British subjects in Munich would be able to leave under his guidance. War broke out, however, and I was unable to get away. After a few months, on November 6, 1914, all Englishmen in Germany were arrested and transferred to an internment camp for British civilians at Ruhleben, in sight of Spandau, near Berlin. I remained there, at the Trotting Race Course, for the duration of the First World War. During the four years I spent there the only books available to us were those we were able to get from the American Y.M.C.A. in Berlin, with the help of which two camp libraries were started, one for fiction and one for reference and scholarly books.

Acting as librarian, I helped to get many books into the camp. (We even had a "Ruhleben Camp" bookplate!) Throughout my internment I collected every possible scrap of paper referring to the camp, in addition to the camp newspapers and magazines, and I had the pleasure of seeing the whole collection smuggled out bit by bit under the noses of the German guards. At the end of the war, I transferred the whole collection, as source material showing how a British township organized itself in a democratic way, to the Harvard Law School Library.

J. Davidson Ketchum, a professor in the Department of Psychology at the University of Toronto and a fellow inmate at Ruhleben, who died in 1962, left material which has just been published as *Ruhleben, a Prison Camp Society*, a volume of 384 pages. It is described by Robert B. MacLeod, professor of psychology at Cornell University, as an important contribution to social psychology and a basic and timeless study of the dynamics of individual and group behavior.

Among the five thousand inhabitants of Ruhleben Camp I met old friends from St. Paul's School and made new ones, including Sir John Balfour, K.C.-M.G., and Henry M. Andrews (the husband of Rebecca West). Others of my friends are now dead, such as John A. Campbell, the architect and designer, and Godfrey Pyke, subject of a monograph by David Lampe, entitled *Pyke, the Unknown Genius*. Pyke, who was then a young undergraduate, had entered Germany from Denmark as a secret correspondent for the *Daily Chronicle* during the early months of the war. Given away by the American representative, he was arrested by the Germans and was held in solitary confinement in Berlin. On arrival at the camp, in February 1915, after some months in prison, he told me that he had saved his sanity only by continuously reciting to himself Lewis Carroll's

The Hunting of the Snark. We nursed him back to health while he was in the Jewish barracks. He changed his quarters and was one of the few civilians to escape to England during the war. J. W. Bernal called him "one of the greatest geniuses of his time." He was closely associated with Lord Mountbatten during the Second World War and sponsored such things as the "Weasel Carrier" and "Habakkuk." After the war he died unfulfilled and unrecognized by his fellow countrymen.

Before leaving the subject of Germany, I must recall some of the customers I met while I was in Munich. One of the most curious and mysterious men was the Reverend William H. Hechler (1845–1931), who was at that time chaplain to the British embassy in Vienna and an eager collector of Luther's publications and other Reformation tracts. He played a great part in the early stage of Zionism and introduced Dr. Theodor Herzl to the Grand Duke of Baden and indirectly to William II, the German Emperor. In the recently published diary of Herzl a great deal can be ascertained about this interesting and unusual personality. A recent publication entitled *Herzl, Hechler, the Grand Duke of Baden and the German Emperor: Documents Found by Hermann and Bessi Ellern* throws fresh light on the history of early Zionism. Forty-eight letters in German, English and French (reproduced in facsimile) from Theodor Herzl, the Grand Duke of Baden, the

Reverend Hechler, William II and the Russian Tsar Nicholas cover the period 1896–1904.

Baron Edmond de Rothschild (1845–1934), who amassed a magnificent collection of forty thousand engravings, as well as woodcut books and illuminated manuscripts, was also a regular customer, and I was able to sell him several fine illuminated manuscripts. At a later date I was invited by his son, Baron James de Rothschild, M.P., to give a valuation of the illuminated manuscripts in his father's mansion in the Faubourg St.-Honoré after his mother's death (June 22, 1935). I was also asked to divide this magnificent collection of manuscripts among Baron Edmond's three children, Baron Maurice de Rothschild, of Paris, who is now dead, Baron James de Rothschild, M.P., who bequeathed all his art objects, library and manuscripts at Tring to the British nation, and Madame Alexandrine de Rothschild. Baron Edmond de Rothschild bequeathed all his forty thousand engravings, as well as his illustrated books, to the Musée du Louvre, in the care of Monsieur André Blum, the honorary curator, who acted as Baron Edmond's expert librarian. When Baron Edmond died (November 2, 1934) he had agreed with his wife (who was to follow her husband eight months later) that his entire collection of engravings would be handed over to the Louvre. However, the collection was installed there only in July 1946, after having been preserved, during the war, in the Château de Valençay.

Among important American collectors, in addition to Mr. Henry Clay Folger, Rosenthals were much appreciated by Mr. Kalbfleisch and Mr. Edward E. Ayer, of Chicago, who gave his magnificent collection of Americana to the Newberry Library; in 1926 or 1927 I was asked by the then director of the Newberry Library to value the Ayer Collection and was able to do so in one afternoon, but I was so overwhelmed by the magnificence of the books he had collected that I was unfit for anything else that afternoon! Mr. Ayer left his superb collection of ornithological books to the Field Museum of Natural History, Chicago. A catalogue of that collection was published in 1926.

Mr. John Pierpont Morgan, Sr. (1837–1913), was another customer. He was rather elusive, and it was necessary, in carrying out a big deal, to see him in person. In April 1912, Heinrich, one of Ludwig Rosenthal's sons, and I left for Aix-les-Bains, at Mr. Morgan's request, in order to show him our greatest treasures in the way of books and manuscripts. We arrived at Aix and arranged to see Mr. Morgan on the following day. However, that very night news of the sinking of the *Titanic* arrived, and it was feared that Mr. J. P. Morgan, Jr., had been on board and had lost his life with so many others. Mr. Morgan, Mr. Rosenthal and I were the only guests at the huge hotel, as it was out of season for taking the waters, but we were unable to meet him. Some months later, arrangements were made to meet him in Paris, and we took our treasured wares with us to

the Hotel Bristol, on the Place Vendôme, where he
was in the habit of staying. On being admitted to
his suite I had the interesting experience of seeing
Mr. Morgan being approached by his usual dealers
in antiques, one of whom seized him by his waistcoat
buttons and held him firmly with both hands so as
not to let him get away. After the departure of the
antique dealers, Mr. Morgan, who was not in a very
favorable mood, examined rather cursorily what we
had displayed on some available tables. He refused
to buy the original manuscript of Mozart's *Concerto
in C* (a priceless treasure, now in Vienna), first
incunable editions of the Hebrew Bible (now almost
as priceless), and other wonderful items. However, he
did buy the unique Verrazano Globe, to which I
have already alluded.

It was in May 1912, when he was seventy-five
years old, that I had the singular pleasure of
selling this most important contribution to the
early history of America to Mr. Morgan personally.
He died in 1913.

The other item I was able to sell Mr. Morgan was
the only surviving copy of one of the earliest German maps of the world. It was apparently designed
by Hanns Ruest in the third quarter of the fifteenth
century at Augsburg and was entirely printed from
one large wood block. The map was preserved by
being pasted inside the inner front cover of a fine
large copy of the 1472 edition of Strabo's *Geography*
in Latin.

In 1923 the Morgan Library was endowed as an

institution for research by his son, John Pierpont
Morgan, Jr., whom I met for the first time in New
York in 1925. I had with me an original red morocco
case containing a number of shelves for a portable
library of small books such as Napoleon Bonaparte
used to take with him, carrying them in his coach
on his campaigns. I presented this case to Mr.
Morgan, and he had the graciousness to accept it as a
personal gift. He did not usually like presents, but
he could not refuse this one, as it bore the initials
J. P. M. (perhaps the initials of one of Napoleon's
generals who also loved books and carried them with
him on foreign conquests in imitation of his master).
The following year I was able to meet in London
Mr. Morgan's librarian, Miss Belle da Costa Greene,
and to accompany her and her mother to Paris.
I still remember Mr. Henry Yates Thompson, the
great collector of illuminated manuscripts, coming
to say goodbye to Miss Greene at Victoria Station
and presenting her with a very fine illuminated
manuscript. On my arrival in Paris I was able to
arrange with Monsieur Girard, librarian of the
Prince de Masséna (a descendant of Napoleon's
famous marshal) to allow me to bring Miss Greene
to visit the Masséna Mansion and show her the
Napoleonic relics and the magnificent Duc de Rivoli
Collection of Venetian woodcut books (now un-
happily scattered all over the world).

Another good client was Mr. Elkan Nathan Adler
(1861–1946), whom I had known since I was five
years old, in Hove. A son of the first English Chief

Rabbi, Dr. Nathan Marcus Adler, and a brother of the second Chief Rabbi, Dr. Hermann Adler, he was an international lawyer, a Hebraist, a historian and a book collector; he was, too, one of the most remarkable men I have ever met. I shall tell more about him later.

Chapter VI

Back in England I was honored with the friendship of the Duke of Alba (1878–1953) and the very talented Spanish Ambassador Merry del Val (d. 1943), who was a brother of the Papal secretary of state and the father of the present Spanish ambassador to the United States. Señor Merry del Val, whenever he had to prepare an important speech, would come to my office to consult the appropriate volumes of *Espasa,* the great Spanish encyclopedia.

Soon after my return to London I was welcomed by the director of a famous bookshop who had already written to me care of the Ruhleben Civilian Internment Camp. He informed me that the firm was waiting for my return to England to engage me to promote their sales of Continental books and develop other specialized branches, which I was to create in the course of some twenty-one years.

Having presented me with a fountain pen and a large, empty desk, he left me to my own devices as to how to begin developing the business in Continental books. To my amazement, during my very first week with the firm I managed to secure a most important customer, who was to prove a source of great strength to the firm.

As the war was over, many Frenchmen came to London to initiate business negotiations with their English colleagues and to begin new relations in their own branches. One afternoon in this first week I was called downstairs to the shop to interpret for a French gentleman who wanted to buy an autograph letter that was displayed in the window and was marked twenty-five shillings. He also wanted to make further inquiries. He gave me his visiting card, which introduced him as Monsieur Eugène Schneider, of Le Creusot. During the First World War, which had just ended, Monsieur Schneider had been a source of strength to the French government and the Allies in general, as he was one of the most important manufacturers of artillery in Europe.

Monsieur Schneider explained to me that as he was married to a lineal descendent of James Fitzjames, Duke of Berwick, the natural son of James II and Arabella Churchill, he would be interested in acquiring any bindings connected with the royal house of Stuart and all interesting manuscript material relating to that family. He promised to return next March. He kept his word, and his first visit resulted in his first large purchase, which amounted to no less than £1,000, a very large sum in those days.

I was glad that owing to my intervention the firm, in the very first week I arrived, had sold goods to a single Continental customer for two and a half times my annual salary. In subsequent years Monsieur Schneider proved to be one of my most faithful customers, and I was able to help him add important items to the family collections.

Another interesting French visitor was Monsieur Louis Barthou, one of the most discriminating connoisseurs among French bibliophiles. A minister in a number of French cabinets over many years, he was in 1919 the minister of justice and as such wielded a great deal of influence. I once was invited to visit his flat in Paris, and there he showed me a magnificent series of original drawings by Victor Hugo to illustrate his novel *Les Travailleurs de la mer*. These vigorous drawings lined the walls of his library, and they were most impressive. On that occasion I enlisted Monsieur Barthou's help in solving a family problem.

A stepbrother of my mother's had, on his death in May 1914, left her a legacy, and this had been sequestrated by the government along with the rest of his fortune, as the greater part of his estate had been bequeathed to the children of his married brother, who had returned to Germany a short time before the outbreak of the First World War. My mother had been unable to obtain possession of the legacy, but after my appeal to Monsieur Barthou the illegal sequestration was lifted and the money duly reached my mother's hands. I feel, however, that I must add here that when I asked Monsieur Barthou to see that justice was done he replied, "Certainly,

I will arrange this, but on all future purchases of autographs from your catalogues you must give me at least fifteen per cent discount." This from the minister of justice!

Luck plays a great part in discoveries. I remember a young man coming to me in 1922 with a pathetic tale of needing money for a short holiday in the south of France. He brought a bundle of odds and ends of leaves of manuscripts and cut-out miniatures, and he explained that he could not get the price he wanted from one or two London dealers whom he had consulted. After looking at them and feeling sorry for him, I gave him what he asked; and I put them aside. Some months later, a young boy of thirteen or fourteen years of age came in. He had a hobby of painting pictures of the saints in medieval style, and he liked to come and inspect European miniatures. I showed him this bundle. He looked through it and suggested that one of the miniatures looked like a Fouquet. I examined it more carefully and to refresh my memory took out the volume of reproductions of the famous forty-four Fouquet miniatures in the museum at Chantilly. The boy was right; this was one of the missing pages in the famous Book of Hours in the collection of the Duc d'Aumale. This miniature of Saint Michael conquering the Demon was subsequently bought by Viscount Bearstead who had despaired of ever getting an authentic painting by Fouquet. No doubt one day it will be left to the nation, which already has one leaf by Fouquet in the British Museum.* This newly discovered miniature has been fully described by Comte Paul Durrieu in a special monograph which was issued in 1923 by the French Society for the Reproduction of Manuscripts, *Livre d'heures peint par Jean Fouquet pour Maître Étienne Chevalier. Le 45ième feuillet de ce Manuscrit retrouvé en Angleterre.*

This young boy, who led me to identify the forty-fifth miniature of Jean Fouquet, came to me, with his mother and grandmother, with whom he lived, to look at early European miniatures. His mother told me that she was concerned about his spending so much time in painting in the style of the early masters and in looking at early Italian paintings in the National Gallery, where he had special pleasure in showing them and explaining them to other children. She was unnecessarily worried at this precocious interest; he was later to be known as a very interesting modernist painter and author—Sir Francis Cyril Rose.

While working at the British Museum at my thesis on Harsha, the seventh-century king of northern India, I made the acquaintance of an extraor-

* A few weeks ago three men were charged with breaking in and stealing six miniature paintings from Upton House, Warwickshire, which is in the hands of the National Trust, though still the residence of Viscount Bearstead's son. Among the six stolen paintings was the St. Michael miniature which was recovered.

dinary-looking young man. He was a Russian, spoke very bad French, was of unprepossessing appearance, with a flattened nose, and looked rather like what I imagine a Tartar would be. He introduced himself and told me his name was Jacques Faitlovitch and that his mission in life was to rescue the Falashas, or black Jews of Abyssinia, from their lowly condition and to bring them back to Judaism. He explained that while he himself was not by any means a conforming Jew, he felt this was his duty to the Falashas, apparently because he had first heard about them in Paris while attending the classes of Professor Joseph Halévy, who had been to Abyssinia many years before, had met some Falashas and had brought back some records of their history and prayers. The reason Faitlovitch came to London was to get in touch with the Chief Rabbi of the time and with some prominent members of the Jewish community. He left after some weeks, deeply disappointed; he had found no help with the scheme, which seemed too fantastic to the English he had met.

Later in Paris in 1903 I met Faitlovitch again, on the eve of his departure for his first visit to Abyssinia. He had been fortunate enough to meet Baron Maurice de Rothschild, who was going to shoot big game in Abyssinia and who promised to take Faitlovitch with him. I remember the small farewell party which a few students and friends, including myself, gave to Faitlovitch before his departure, when he was solemnly presented with an early nineteenth-century horse pistol for his protection on the expedition. As is now well known, Faitlovitch's first journey was successful and was followed by many others; young Falashas have now been trained for some time both in Paris and Eritrea and most recently in Israel.

While I was still in Munich a letter arrived from a London firm by the name of Epworth and Company, with offices in Newman Street, inquiring for medical, pharmaceutical and other scientific manuscripts. At the time, in the stock of Ludwig Rosenthal there were masses of such manuscripts, of varying degrees of interest and all manner of dates. Very soon case after case left Munich for London. We were puzzled that a firm not in the *Booksellers' Directory* should need such quantities of manuscripts, for which they paid considerable sums in the course of some years. On my next visit to London I called at Newman Street; the offices of Epworth and Company seemed to be one room on the second floor, and I was informed by the caretaker that the owner of the firm visited his office only to fetch letters and parcels. I looked through the letter box and saw nothing but bare walls. The firm remained most mysterious, till one day some book was returned by them and I found that the paper used for packing came from Burroughs, Wellcome and Company, the famous manufacturers of Tabloids and other medicines.

Later, on my return to London, after the First World War, while passing the chemist shop of Bell & Croydon, I found that there was an entrance, in the basement, to a Medical Historical Museum open only to medical men. I visited the basement and was amazed at the marvelous exhibits there of medical antiquity and interest. I soon met Dr. C. J. S. Thompson, the author of a number of popular works, such as *The Mystery and Romance of Alchemy and Pharmacy* (1897), and found that he was the director and librarian of Sir Henry Solomon Wellcome, the owner of Burroughs, Wellcome and Company, multi-millionaire and collector of everything that pertained to the human body. After a time Dr. Thompson confessed that he had figured as "Epworth and Company," one of the pseudonyms behind which Sir Henry liked to hide for the purpose of buying. Over many years I was able to supply Sir Henry with wonderful items which now figure in the great building of the Wellcome Historical Museum and in the Wellcome Historical Library, in Euston Road, a monument to Sir Henry's collecting.

Sir Henry Solomon Wellcome (1853–1936) was a manufacturing chemist and patron of science, of American descent. Born in a log cabin at Almond, Wisconsin, the younger son of Solomon Cummings Wellcome, farmer and itinerant missionary among the Dakota Indians, he spent much of his boyhood under the influence of William W. Mayo, in Garden City, Minnesota. At the age of twenty-one he came to England, where he met another American by birth, S. M. Burroughs, and founded the firm of Burroughs, Wellcome and Company. With his partner, he manufactured fine chemicals and became famous for "Tabloids," which he patented, a special kind of combined drugs in small glass bottles with screw tops which had the advantage of being easily carried in a man's pocket or in a lady's handbag. After his partner's death, in 1895, Wellcome became the sole owner of the business, which brought him great wealth. In 1913 he came out into the open and founded the Wellcome Historical Medical Museum, for which he had been collecting secretly for many years. Nothing human was alien to his collecting. At his death he left a house entirely filled with various kinds of perambulators (a burden for his trustees) and immense collections of Egyptian antiques, amulets of all kinds, paintings of medical interest, portraits, engravings, and many thousands of manuscripts and books of medical and scientific interest. He liked having goods in quantities. Once, by accident, a telegram from Constantinople reached me which was signed by one of his corps of traveling agents—he had just bought an entire Turkish pharmacy because of the collection of ancient druggists' jars.

At first a portion of his treasures was housed in the basement of Bell & Croydon, one of the chemist shops which he owned in Wigmore Street, in the West End of London; but his great museum was later opened in Euston Road, in an enormous building which was specially erected for that purpose by him. The world was amazed to see what he had amassed by means of his great fortune during many years.

He left the whole of his immense wealth for research and education. He encouraged archaeology in Africa and Palestine. He was an ardent supporter of Sir Henry Stanley, the journalist who went to Africa to search for the medical missionary Dr. Livingston.

In 1901 he married a daughter of the great and justly famous philanthropist Thomas John Barnardo (1845–1905), who was the founder of the "Dr. Barnardo's Homes."* Over ninety homes and agencies for destitute boys and girls were founded or maintained by him.

A remarkable and unusual customer was Mr. Harry Price (1881–1948), the author of a number of best-sellers on haunted rectories and other occult subjects. A wealthy industrialist, he was keenly interested in magic and psychical phenomena and managed to amass one of the best-known collections on conjuring, stage illusions, mesmerism, spiritualism and all forms of occult activities. On his death he bequeathed this magnificent library (of which there is now an excellent catalogue) to London University. At first he was a fervent disbeliever in all occult manifestations, but he gave one the feeling, after many years of investigations with all kinds of machinery devised to catch fraudulent and unwary mediums, that he had begun to believe in some forms of telepathy and spirits.

* She later became Mrs. Somerset Maugham and was subsequently the object of her author-husband's bitter attacks.

Another interesting collector, but in a different way, was Mr. Edward Frederick Phelips (1852–1928). This very charming, but shy, gentleman had been a poorly paid clerk in the City of London, always dreaming of Spain but never able to realize his wish to visit that country. One day, when he was already middle-aged, a distant relative left him a small fortune, and he was then able to indulge his fancy and buy books about Spain, especially about Madrid. He soon got to know all the streets in Madrid, their names and their past history, and it was in his behalf that I was able to buy from Señor Emilio Cotarelo, secretary of the Spanish Academy, his remarkable collection of Madrid maps, which Mr. Phelips ultimately bequeathed with the rest of his library (known as the Eliot-Phelips Collection) to the Guildhall Library, in the City of London. It is at present on loan to the University of London.

Mr. Phelips and I met one year in Madrid, and I was able to introduce him to the most famous Spanish collector, Don Felix Boix, general manager of the Northern Spanish Railways and a leading member of the Sociedad de Amigos de Arte. In addition to an exceptional collection of original drawings by Spanish artists and a beautiful library of rare Spanish books in contemporary morocco bindings, Señor Boix had the finest possible collection of Spanish court almanacs in magnificent signed bindings. Señor Boix was so impressed by the knowledge and love of Mr. Phelips for Madrid that he presented him on his very first visit with his most beautiful *guia,* a splendid token of Spanish generosity.

As I was recently informed by Mr. A. H. Hall, Librarian of the Guildhall Library, Mr. Phelips became the heir to the great Elizabethan Mansion of Montacute, Somerset, which is now vested in the National Trust to be safeguarded as a National Monument.

Full details of the family are available in Burke's Landed Gentry of Great Britain, 1937 edition, volume 2, pp. 1797–8.

Among other English bibliophiles of the period were John Burns* and Sir Hugh Seymour Walpole.† Both were eager collectors. Mr. Burns, the labor leader and sometime president of the Board of Trade, was particularly interested in Sir Thomas More and his *Utopia.* He succeeded in buying all editions and all translations of the *Utopia* except one, in addition to a series of famous *Chronicles of England* and the principal books on the City of London. When I asked him why he was so fascinated by Thomas More and the *Utopias,* Mr. Burns replied that when he was a poor workingman he picked up from a bookstall for sixpence a modern reprint of the *Utopia* and was so affected by the contents that he determined that if

* John Burns (1858–1943), Member of Parliament for Battersea from 1892 to 1918; cabinet minister from 1905 to 1914, when he resigned in protest against Britain's declaration of war.

† Hugh Walpole (1884–1941), very successful author of forty-eight novels and several plays.

he ever had any money he would buy every edition that was available. Mrs. Burns, however, was not so keen on her husband's book collecting, and he had to await her annual departure on holiday and then summon taxis in order to be able to collect his purchases over many months from those of the London booksellers whom he patronized. Mr. Burns was full of interesting stories; he explained how he had invented the description "liquid history" for the River Thames when showing a party of Australians over the House of Commons. He also used to tell a story of King Edward VII and himself: When asked by the King why he was in the habit of talking to the Chinese ambassador, Mr. Burns replied that he did so because it was unusual to find that rare combination of good manners and love of truth at a court.

In the course of many years I met the notorious Thomas James Wise numberless times, but had very little conversation with him, as he was exclusively interested in English literature. He seemed to me a genial, very pleasant man, good company, though inclined to be vain. But in the eyes of people connected with the book trade he had every right to be proud of himself. He had produced some two hundred and fifty privately printed reprints of small and rare pieces and had published at his own expense more than twenty important bibliographies of English authors with full collations and notes (sometimes only one hundred copies of each were printed), to say nothing of his enormous eleven-volume catalogue of his collection, known as the Ashley Library.

He was born in 1859 and died in 1937 and is described by Mr. Arundell Esdaile in the *Dictionary of National Biography* as "Book Collector, Bibliographer, Editor and Forger." At the time I knew him the last of these four professions was certainly not known to anyone.

At an early age Mr. Wise, who had started life from humble beginnings, visited bookshops and was so enchanted with what he found that after some time he made a practice of trying to find out what had happened to the families or heirs of English poets and endeavored to buy from them all the manuscripts and work specimens left by the poets, thus setting a fashion now followed in a stupendous way by the University of Texas.

When the Shelley and Browning societies were formed in London in 1886, Wise was entrusted with the printing of the Shelley Society's publications. Soon he had gathered sufficient funds to begin to buy all English poets and not a few prose writers. His library (when sold by his widow in 1937 to the British Museum in accordance with the directions given in his will) was "in 16th and 17th century writers of moderate, in the late 17th and 18th century very great, and in the 19th century of unapproached completeness."

At the death of the poet Swinburne in 1909 Mr. Wise hastened to buy from Mr. W. T. Watts-Dunton (who had befriended and protected the poet) whatever he wanted of Swinburne's library and manuscripts.

Mr. Wise, in my presence, used to boast of his efforts to show up literary forgeries, especially in the way of forged autograph letters of Thackeray and other nineteenth-century authors. I heard him say that in one case, when appealed to by an American collector, he had taken alleged autograph letters of Thackeray and torn them up in front of a London bookseller who had had them manufactured. No one had any doubt about the seriousness of Mr. Thomas James Wise.

However, in 1934, three years before his death, Messrs. John Carter and Graham Pollard announced in *The Times Literary Supplement* that they had had grave doubts as to the authenticity of a number of nineteenth-century literary pamphlets; and they promised early publication of proofs on which they had based their theory. No mention was made of Mr. Wise's name or any other suspect in their article.

Not long after the publication of that article, Messrs. Carter and Pollard published *An Enquiry into the Nature of Certain Nineteenth Century Pamphlets,* which proved that some forty to fifty pieces commanding high prices, both in the auction rooms and at booksellers', were forgeries, many being dated earlier than the known first editions, and all by type, paper or imprint were less than genuine and were accordingly traced back to Wise.

During the course of years he had gradually sold a

number of copies of each of these pamphlets through
an ex-clerk in his oil business whom he had helped
to start as a bookseller. Since the appearance of the
Enquiry more pamphlets have been definitely shown
to be forgeries from the same source, and Wise has
now been most clearly exposed as having habitually
sold books or rare documents which he had had
forged, and which were therefore worthless, at high
prices to collectors and to booksellers whom he advised and who had trusted him. He was especially
guilty in selling regularly these no longer doubtful
books to Mr. John Henry Wrenn, whose large collection of English literature, now in the University of
Texas Library, is the only one to contain all of
Wise's forged pamphlets.

Since Mr. Arundell Esdaile's article appeared in
the volume of the *Dictionary of National Biography*
it has been proved, without a shadow of doubt, that
Mr. Wise was guilty not only of forgery but of theft,
especially from the collection of the early English
plays in the British Museum, where he had special
privileges of consulting their treasures and was
trusted and advised by Dr. Richard Garnett and Mr.
Alfred Pollard, who occupied high positions in that
institution. Mr. Wise, when he needed pages to complete imperfect English plays in his own library,
simply stole them from the British Museum copies.

It is difficult to understand his mentality and
the motives which removed him from the ranks
of straightforward and honest bibliophiles, especially
when one considers that he was a man of means,

that he was a devoted lover of literature and bibliography, and that he intended his collection to be incorporated after death in the British Museum library, which he had ransacked for pages to fill gaps in the copies in his own possession.

In the course of his collecting he seems to have impressed Colonel Wilkinson of the Worcester College Library, Oxford, with the possibility that he would leave his library to Worcester College. He was therefore made an honorary Master of Arts at Oxford and a Fellow of Worcester College!

Some five or six years before the Second World War, by an extraordinary combination of circumstances, I was able to compile a special catalogue, of which only a few copies were issued, containing no less than five complete block books. My idea was to endeavor to sell the set as a whole. What was my surprise one morning, therefore, to greet an old customer, Mr. R. E. Hart, who had been in the habit of buying moderately priced but interesting old books which contained woodcut illustrations, armed with a proposition to buy the collection as a whole at a slightly reduced figure. He was carrying a small leather bag, such as businessmen were wont to do in those Edwardian days. Our customer's proposition was accepted, and he thereupon produced no less than £25,000 in one-pound notes, which occupied two cashiers a considerable time in counting. He explained the reason for this form of payment: he did not wish his bankers to know that he was spending so much money on books. The gentleman in question was a leading director of British Ropes.*

After his death, in 1946, the five block books, together with his magnificent collection of other early products of the printing press, went to the library of his alma mater, Cambridge University. Mr. Hart's bequest included a perfect copy of Raoul Lefèvre's *History of Jason,* printed by William Caxton at Westminster; it had come from the famous Harleian Library. The five block books in the bequest consisted of a *Biblia Pauperum,* with German text, which formerly had been in the ducal library at Gotha (now in East Germany), and four important volumes from the famous monastery library at Göttweig, in Austria —a Latin edition of the *Biblia Pauperum,* the *Ars moriendi,* the Apocalypse, and an *Ars memorandi* similar to the (incomplete) copy sold in the Newberry Library sale at Sotheby's in November 1965 for £29,500. Needless to say, all the block books bequeathed by Mr. Hart were in fine condition and quite complete.

During the Second World War, when I had left London because of the Nazi bombing, I was happy to move to temporary quarters in a fifteenth-century house in Oxford, my old university. I was delighted to find that my friend and lawyer, Mr. James P. R. Lyell, whom I had known for over twenty years, was living in a charming old house, The Knoll, at Abing-

* British Ropes is now the world's largest integrated manufacturer of ropes, wire and allied products.

don. In consequence, nearly every Sunday afternoon saw me in the Oxford omnibus on my way to Abingdon, where Mr. and Mrs. Lyell awaited me for tea and where I had long talks with Mr. Lyell about his library. This eminent solicitor had begun a number of collections. He had succeeded in amassing a remarkable quantity of books and proclamations on the Spanish Armada, both in English and in Spanish, which he sold, in July 1939, when he was tired of them, to Mr. Thomas W. Lamont, of the J. P. Morgan bank, who presented them to the Harvard College Library.

In the *Harvard Library Notes,* No. 30 (March 1940), pages 303–307, the late famous bibliographer and librarian of Harvard, Mr. William A. Jackson, described this collection very briefly. In all, the gift comprised nine contemporary manuscripts and sixty-four books printed before 1640. According to Mr. Jackson, the collection given by Mr. Lamont not only might well induce the reappraisal of the story of the Spanish Armada of 1588, but also might be the means of inspiring an interest in history itself.

Among the manuscripts was a fine contemporary map from John Mountgomery's *Treatise of the Navy,* dated 1574 and especially transcribed for Henry Percy, the "Wizard" Earl of Northumberland, who served against the Armada.

Included in the gift are signed documents showing the extent of King Philip II's efforts, one being an order to the authorities in Peru to send contributions of gold and silver for the fitting out of the Spanish ships, and others illustrating the organization of the English defense by the Lord High Admiral, Charles Lord Howard of Effingham.

The earliest printed document is the copy of the Bull of Pope Pius V, published in 1570, excommunicating Queen Elizabeth. This appears to be an example of the edition which John Felton obtained from the Spanish ambassador's chaplain and which he nailed to the door of the palace of the Bishop of London.

In addition to a number of propaganda publications contemporary with the Armada issued by both the English and the Spanish, there is an extraordinary item in the shape of a broadside poster, printed in Seville, dated September 5, 1588, announcing the triumph of the Spanish Fleet, the invasion of England and the capture of Drake. This poster was evidently destined to be placarded all over Spain, but only one other copy besides the Harvard copy is known to survive.

Mr. James P. R. Lyell spent many years in making this unique collection, now one of Harvard's most prized possessions.

Mr. Lyell made a collection of Cervantes, English books printed by Catholics abroad, a fine series of bibliographies, and a beautiful library of early English literature and first editions. He decided, after some of our talks, to change his line of collecting; and, through me, he gradually disposed of the major part of his books, both Spanish and English. He used the proceeds to start a new collection of important manuscripts, which he bequeathed to the Bodleian Library, Oxford, as well as a large sum of money to endow a professorship (the first in England, I believe) of bibliography; the first holder of the chair is Professor N. R. Ker.

Not only was Mr. Lyell one of the chief collectors in England of Spanish books, but although he could not speak the language, he even traveled to Spain, where he impressed the dealers with his great knowledge of their wares. He will be remembered, in addition to his munificence to the University of Oxford, for his great work on Spanish illustrated books entitled *Early Book Illustration in Spain*. This was published at his own expense in 1926, with 248 illustrations, in 500 copies. It at once became a standard bibliography. His other publication, a monograph on the founder of the University of Alcalá de Henares and the creator of the first great Polyglot Bible, Cardinal Francisco Ximénez de Cisneros, Archbishop of Toledo (born in 1436, died in 1517), is extremely useful and contains a census of the copies of the famous Polyglot Bible.

Chapter VII

One night during the Second World War an old
friend of mine, Dr. Cecil Roth, then a lecturer in
post-Biblical Jewish studies at Oxford, dropped in at
my quarters to show me a remarkable letter. The
hour was late, and he had just returned from London, where he had given one of his weekly lectures;
but he could not wait to discuss the letter, which he
had just received. It was written on very beautiful
deckle-edged paper and was signed by a gentleman
who was the brother of an English ambassador and
was himself a member of a very old and important
English banking firm. Enclosed with the letter was a
typed catalogue of some remarkable Hebrew incunabula, including all the greatest rarities, such as
the 1475 *Rashi* (the first book printed in Hebrew)
and—the greatest treasure of all—the only illustrated
Hebrew incunable, the famous *Mashal Hakadmoni*.

The writer of the letter, although unknown to Dr.
Roth, had written in terms of greatest affection. He
was seeking Dr. Roth's opinion as to the authenticity
of the catalogued items before consummation of
negotiations for their acquisition. It was a fantasti-
cally improbable project, and the explanation was,

for the moment, beyond us. Dr. Roth and I arranged to visit the headquarters of the eminent gentleman who had sent the list. And there the mystery was quickly solved:

The late Elkan Nathan Adler (whom I have already mentioned) was the greatest collector of Hebrew and Jewish books in England. He had studied at London University and after taking his degree had devoted himself to the law and in time had become the senior partner in the firm of Adler and Perowne, Solicitors, in the City of London. He also was one of the pioneers in English-Jewish historical research and from 1912 to 1914 was president of the Jewish Historical Society of England. A bachelor, he was able to make frequent journeys abroad, often in behalf of Jewish charitable organizations; and wherever he was he visited bookshops and the owners of fine libraries. With his family connections and with his considerable income, he was able to acquire thousands of rare books and, above all, rare manuscripts— not only Judaica, but also world literature in general. In Egypt, on one of his many journeys, he managed to acquire a large number of fragments of Hebrew manuscripts from Fostat, the ancient capital; at the same time he acquired some important Greek papyri.

As described in *Essays in Memory of E. N. Adler* (1948), by the Reverend Ephraim Levine, "he was a discriminating collector, with an eye that roved over literature, anxious to acquire and treasure first editions and rare books in any language. Books were his friends. His idea of friendship, which he carried out in his human contacts, was transferred to his library, and he knew the contents as well as the title pages of his books. To say that he was well read would be but a poor tribute to his knowledge. His was one of those minds that seem to store up knowledge of all kinds and to be able to bring it to the surface." Among my own private treasures is a fine head-and-shoulders portrait of him painted by Pilichowski. In the 1920's he was forced by circumstances to sell his entire Jewish library; it went to the Jewish Theological Seminary of New York for £25,000, which was paid to Mr. Adler by the great American philanthropist Jacob Schiff. However, time and circumstances allowed Mr. Adler to start collecting again, and in 1939 he had collected quite a large number of printed books and manuscripts, which filled the shelves of his house in Porchester Terrace.

One day, during a game of bridge with some male friends Mr. Adler, who was then in his eighties, said, "I still have a magnificent collection of early printed books"; and when asked whether he would sell them he said, "I would sell my incunables, which are worth £8000"—forgetting, however, that nearly all the incunables he now had were incomplete or in some other way defective. He was asked for a list, and he instructed a typist to type one. It had been his custom to list, in a copy of Moïse Schwab's *Les Incunables hébreux*, not only the items that he had acquired, but also items that he would like to have; now he gave the Schwab book to the typist, who listed all the items written there.

It was in this way that one of his cardplayer friends undertook to purchase Mr. Adler's collection. On his way home, this friend visited a bar and there agreed to resell the collection to an acquaintance whom he had met by chance. That acquaintance then made contact with the gentleman who wrote to Dr. Roth. At our interview with the distinguished gentleman, when the name of Elkan Adler was mentioned I was immediately able to solve the problem. Dr. Roth and I thereafter had nothing further to do with the matter.

The final episode was even more remarkable. Purchaser number two repudiated his bargain, and purchaser number one also wished to repudiate his bargain, as the incunabula in question were for the most part very defective, but Elkan Adler contented him by substituting some of his oil paintings. Today, of course, thirty years later, the books would all have been regarded as bargains at the price asked by Mr. Adler.

Our suspicions had first been aroused when, on the day following the arrival of the first letter in Oxford, a friend of purchaser number one rang up Dr. Roth from London and tried to interest him in a unique collection of Hebrew incunabula, though he had no idea what the word meant. It was, of course, a time when people were everywhere buying anything in order to sell at a profit.

As a footnote to this curious affair, I may add that Mr. Adler did manage to sell his incunabula to a third person and that after his death it was found that he had bequeathed all his manuscripts and any book of which there was not a copy on the shelves of the Jewish Theological Seminary to the authorities in New York in gratitude for their having helped him at a difficult period of his life. Mr. Adler's heirs charged me to dispose of the remaining very interesting and very valuable part of his collection.

In the early 1920's, that is to say a few years after the end of the First World War, a very curious situation was created for the firm of booksellers with which I was then connected.

An unknown personage wrote from Belgium a long letter giving information that he had for sale a very important collection of rare autographs. Among the items was a lengthy autograph discourse by Martin Luther and a document signed by Charles the Great. The list contained many other interesting items, but none as unusual as these.

In due course he was answered and was asked for prices. He replied that it was difficult for him to name prices, but that he was anxious to sell; in token of his confidence in us he at once sent the Luther autograph for our inspection to prove the authenticity of his manuscripts.

Needless to say, no document signed by Charles the Great, or Charlemagne, has ever appeared in the autograph market. The lengthy and important

Luther document duly arrived; it was obviously quite authentic, and the price named by its owner was not excessive.

To see whether this manuscript had been published, a member of the staff was sent to the British Museum to call for the complete edition of Luther's works and to see if he could find it therein. He returned with the appalling news that the manuscript not only had been published but was listed as being in the possession of the Marburg Museum. Thereupon a letter was written to the director of the Marburg Museum informing him that this manuscript of Luther, which was listed as being in his museum, had been offered for sale, that we wished to know whether his museum had sold the manuscript, and that in the meantime it was being held at his disposal.

By return of post an express letter arrived from the Marburg director informing us that the manuscript indeed belonged to the museum and had been stolen, and asking for further information. We gave particulars of the man who had offered us the manuscript for sale, together with a further list of manuscripts he had offered us in the meantime.

At the request of the Marburg Museum we returned the manuscript by registered post to the authorities. What was our amazement, however, a week or so later, when my chief, on leaving the dining room of the club where we used to lunch, was accosted in the hall by an individual who pressed a piece of paper on him—a summons to appear before a judge in chambers (it was midsummer) to answer a suit instituted by the German Embassy in London for the return of all the manuscripts which they alleged were in our hands and which had been listed in the first letter from Brussels. This was a remarkable specimen of German gratitude for our efforts to restore supposedly stolen property to a German museum.

We had no difficulty in disposing of the accusation, and we heard no more of the matter. But discreet inquiries shortly afterward produced a very different picture. The manuscripts in question, which had been on exhibition in the Marburg Museum and had disappeared from their showcases, had been removed without any degree of violence. They had been secretly taken away to Belgium for the purpose of selling them and buying rifles and ammunition to equip one of the many right-wing conspiracies against the Weimar Republic. Needless to say, nothing of these events appeared in the German or other press!

A few years ago an Italian catalogue of antiquarian books came into my hands. As a rule, few Italian booksellers issued catalogues of sufficient interest for me to read them through very carefully, but in this case my attention was caught by a description of a Ferrara Spanish Bible printed on "caerulean" paper. The price was not excessive, the binding was described as being of interest, and I telegraphed for the book. What was my surprise when I was able to welcome the arrival of an extraordinarily large-sized original Ferrara Spanish Bible, printed by the famous Usque printer at Ferrara, dedicated to the remarkable stateswoman Donna Gracia of Naxos, printed throughout on darkish-blue paper as fresh as if it had come from the printer's the day before and in a remarkably fine Italian contemporary gilt binding. On checking the only complete checklist of Ferrara Bibles, by Professor Stanley Rypins, I found that he had listed one large-paper copy of this book, the only copy known to him (obviously a presentation copy), in the Bologna Library. I was thunderstruck by the mention of this copy and was terrified to think that this book might have been pilfered from the Bologna Library. How great, therefore, was my relief when I read in Professor Rypins' description that the Bologna copy had several pages damaged by fire and, on looking them up in the new arrival, found that these pages were absolutely intact. This Bible, fully described in a catalogue, has now found a permanent resting place among the rare books in the Philadelphia Public Library. The acquisition was due to the eagle eye of Miss Ellen Schaffer, the custodian of rare books at Philadelphia, whom I had formerly met at the Henry E. Huntington Library, at San Marino, California.

Chapter VIII

Through my long friendship with King Manuel of Portugal, I was able to obtain for the London firm with which I was then connected a whole series of "royal appointments"—first of all, that of King Manuel himself; of his wife, Queen Victoria; then of his mother, Queen Amélie, the widow of King Carlos I. After the publication of the first volume of his catalogue, King Manuel at his weekly luncheon at Buckingham Palace asked King George V to appoint the firm as his booksellers, to which King George readily agreed.

The Duke of Windsor, then Prince of Wales, began to visit the premises, and he told us that his grandfather King Edward VII had left the library at Marlborough House bookless and that the shelves were lined simply by rows of imitation book backs in leather, but no books. As the Prince did not wish to incur the ridicule of his visitors, he wanted to fill the shelves and bought a great many works on history and collections of memoirs.

At about the same time the firm also began to sell to the late Princess Royal and her husband the late Earl of Harewood. He was chiefly interested in

Masonic bindings, and the Princess Royal used to buy the same kind of books as presents for her husband.

How did I manage to meet King Manuel? In the autumn of 1913, among the foreign visitors to Munich was the young ex-king Manuel of Portugal (1889–1932), who came to Munich on his honeymoon, for the Festival Season of Wagner Opera. He had married, September 4, Princess Augusta Victoria, daughter of Prince Wilhelm of Hohenzollern, whose ancient castle was at Sigmaringen. As I thought he would be rather bored during a prolonged stay in Munich I wrote to him quoting a few books on Portugal that were in stock. He came at once after receiving the letter and proved to be a most charming and amiable young man, who enjoyed speaking French, the language of his mother, who was born Princess Amélie d'Orléans.

Soon after the Armistice of November 1918, when it was possible to leave Ruhleben Camp, I returned to England and plunged at once into the London world of antiquarian books. In January 1919 I wrote to King Manuel, who by then had settled down in his own house at Twickenham, and he came to see me and confided to me his secret project of writing an authoritative, detailed monograph on the life and reign of his namesake and predecessor, the famous King Manuel I, the Fortunate, under whose reign at the end of the fifteenth century and the beginning of the sixteenth, Portugal had been at the height of her glory in empire, literature and art. In order to be able to write this work it was necessary to collect the appropriate material and King Manuel decided to endeavor to obtain every book printed in Portugal even before Manuel I came to the throne and up to 1600. As he himself was unable to visit his native land, this meant frequent visits on my part to Portugal in his behalf and also to Spain. During these journeys I was able to see a great deal of these two countries, and my affection for them and their peoples grew considerably.

From 1919 to 1932 I spent much time in searching for the necessary Portuguese source material for the King. Owing to the breaking up of some famous libraries, such as those of the Conde de Ameal, Antonio Augusto de Carvalho Monteiro, Azevedo-Samodaes and many others, it was possible to obtain books which had not been seen on the book market for fifty or a hundred years, for the royal collection at Twickenham. King Manuel was in this way so fortunate in his purchases that after a few years I made the suggestion to him that he should let the world know of his acquisitions and publish a "short-title catalogue" of his marvelous collection. In November 1925 the King began to work on a catalogue and a year later made up his mind to publish it. However, instead of making a dry bibliography or short-title catalogue of his books, he used this opportunity to show the past glories of Portugal by describing each book not only bibliographically but also with an essay on the author and the subject of the book in its relation to Portuguese history and literature and its contribution to civilization in general.

During my absences from England, King Manuel started writing to me about his catalogue and the rare books which he wished to find or about which I was able to tell him. Also when King Manuel was away from England, either for his yearly cure at Vichy or on a visit to the parents of his wife in Sigmaringen, he wrote to me regularly. Some one hundred or more of these letters, written in French or English, were published in 1957 by the Fundação da Casa de Braganza, in Lisbon, the owners of the copyright; edited with a preface by Professor M. B. Amzalak, formerly Rector of the Universidad Tecnica de Lisboa, they form a volume of some ninety-one quarto pages, with facsimiles of a few letters, and show how King Manuel was interested in the slightest detail connected with his books.*

He used to write (in Portuguese) an essay on each book separately and bring it to me to be typed and for me to make any possible suggestions, bibliographical or literary, on his work. Although I examined each of these bibliographical essays as critically as possible. I could not find anything wrong

* The reader will find on pages 195–207 of this volume extracts in translation from several of King Manuel's letters to me, selected for the way in which they show the immense effort the King put into his bibliographical essays. Permission to use these letters has very kindly been given by Senhor Antonio Luis Gomes, President of the Administrative Council of the Fundação da Casa de Braganza.

with them. As a matter of fact, some of the suggestions presented for the first time by King Manuel were, at a later date, adopted by Portuguese bibliographers. Even when it was a matter of books on astronomy—and on my advice the essay was shown to an eminent English astronomer for his criticism—nothing was found wrong with it. Again, when in the case of the first two books the King possessed, namely two Hebrew incunables printed in Lisbon in 1489, the King's work was submitted to Elkan Nathan Adler, that leading English expert on such books could not find anything wrong, but, on the contrary, accepted various original suggestions by the King about the early printing of Hebrew books in Portugal.

After each essay had been typed it was returned to the King, who revised it a second and sometimes a third time. In Volume 3 (pages 476–477) of his *Catalogue of Portuguese Books* (published posthumously in 1935), a facsimile of one of these manuscripts with corrections and revisions was included, at my suggestion, to show the world that King Manuel was indeed the sole author of this catalogue. In the same way, the King read the proofs that came from the Cambridge University Press and revised them extensively; again a facsimile of such a corrected proof is shown in Volume 3. King Manuel's plan was to have in his library every book printed in Portugal before 1600, and he was successful in making a unique collection of books from 1920 to 1932. (He died on July 2, 1932.)

King Manuel was particularly happy that Dr. Oliveira Salazar, head of the Portuguese government, was generous enough to return from the National Library of the Palace of Ajuda several early and exceedingly rare books which his ancestor King Luis had bought by means of his privy purse. King Manuel showed his nobility by bequeathing not only his fortune, but also all his books, to the people of Portugal. They are now kept in a specially guarded library strongroom in the ancient ancestral palace of the Braganzas, at Vilha-Viçoça.

I would like to emphasize once more that the whole of the descriptions of the books as printed in Volumes 1 and 2 was entirely written by King Manuel (and by no one else). The King was kind enough to mention my services to him (much against my desire) in the preface to Volume I of his great *Catalogue*. He also mentions my services in letters to the Conde de Mafra, dated December 31, 1927, August 30, 1929, and November 6, 1929. These letters, of which I knew nothing at the time, were published in *Cartas d'El-Rei D.Manuel II,* by Antonio Cabral, in 1933.

After King Manuel's death and after his will had been duly studied, I was enabled, in order to pay a fitting tribute to his memory, to exhibit some of his rarest books and specimens of his cataloguing and pages of proof of the *Catalogue* corrected by him, in London and in Paris.

In London, I regret to say, visitors were few, but in Paris, when the exhibition was held in the *grande semaine* in June 1934, *tout Paris* arrived in hundreds at the inauguration by President Albert Lebrun at the invitation of Senhor Armando da Gama Ochoa, the Portuguese minister plenipotentiary. The President arrived punctually at three o'clock (the traffic in the one-way street having been entirely reversed by the police) accompanied by Monsieur Julien Cain, Administrator of the National Library, with Sir George Clark, the British ambassador, as well as the ministers of Argentina, Spain, Canada, Finland, Ireland, Colombia, Persia and Ethiopia, and other diplomats representing Nicaragua, Switzerland, Greece, Rumania and Monaco. Miss Margery Withers, the late King's librarian, acted as guide and showed President Lebrun some of the most interesting books and manuscripts collected by the King.

Among the nondiplomat visitors at the inauguration were Her Royal Highness the Infanta Eulalia (daughter of Queen Isabella II of Spain and sister of King Alfonso XII), Princesses de Faucigny-Lucinge, M. Galitzine, de Robech, d'Arenberg, Lucien Murat; Duchesses de La Force, de Cadaval, de Gramont; also Princes Obolensky, de Robech, Galitzine, de Polignac, de Clermont-Tonnerre; the Duke de Gramont; and many other French titled people. Among authors present were Francis Carco and Paul Valéry. All in all, it was an apotheosis of the *grande semaine* of the Paris season of 1934.

Nine years earlier some of the King's books had already been seen in Paris. In March 1925, in the new rooms of a friendly dealer, the opportunity had been taken to organize at the same time an exhibition of first editions of Ronsard and an exhibition of most of the early editions of Luiz Vaz de Camoëns, Portugal's foremost poet. King Manuel, at my request, opened the exhibition in the presence of the British ambassador, the Earl of Cromer. Having made an appointment to meet the King at the same spot a few afternoons later, I found myself, shortly before the appointed time, in the shop of a bookseller who offered me a magnificent, beautifully colored Portuguese portolano, or world chart, on vellum of the sixteenth century. I bought this on the spot without further ado and found that I was going to be late for my appointment with King Manuel. I heard afterward that he had been walking up and down, evidently furious at my lack of punctuality, but when I came into the room where he was waiting I placed the portolano on the floor before him and said, "Your Majesty, I am placing the world at your feet." Immediately he forgot his annoyance, and he bought the portolano, which was obviously the product of an anonymous Portuguese cartographer of great talent.

This portolano figured among the magnificent early manuscript portolanos and maps at the splendid Henry the Navigator Exhibition of 1960, in Lisbon. It was described as "No. 39 Anonimo— Sebastião Lopes, Carta Nautica, ca. 1570. Illuminated on vellum 842 × 1045 mm. The oldest known work of Sebastian Lopes in 1558. He is mentioned in documents of 1582, 1586 and 1587 and from another document it is supposed that he died in 1596 or earlier."

In an introduction to the Catalogue of the Prince Henry the Navigator Exhibition, Senhor Avelino Teixeira da Motta points out that this beautiful map was described for the first time and attributed to Sebastião Lopes in Volume IV of the *Portugaliae Monumenta Cartographica* (Lisbon, 1960).

In this great work the King's magnificent map is reproduced in excellent monochrome on a plate extending over two folio pages. This reproduction does not, of course, show the exquisite coloring of the original, but it gives an excellent idea of the great amount of territory first discovered by the Portuguese and developed by them. Senhor Avelino Teixeira da Motta also gives a long description of this map and of the whole work of Sebastião Lopes.

It was a matter of great satisfaction to me that this chance discovery of mine in a Paris bookshop should prove of such great importance in the history of Portuguese cartography. It is not correct, as suggested by Senhor Avelino Teixeira da Motta, that the map came from the collection of the Comte de Chambord (Henri V of France). There were no maps of any kind in that collection.

In 1926, on a visit to Lisbon, I was offered the library of Antonio Augusto de Carvalho Monteiro (1850–1920), a Portuguese collector who was born in Rio de Janeiro and died at his extraordinary home in Cintra, near Lisbon. (His librarian and secretary, Bernardino Domingos Madeira, later became a close friend; and this friendship, after his early death, was extended to his talented family.)

Carvalho Monteiro was supposed to have been very poor but managed in the course of a lifetime to become extremely rich and was an unusually devoted collector of Camoëns. He even smoked a special brand of "Camoëns" cigars. I succeeded in buying his rarest books, including the first edition (1587) of the comedies of Camoëns and Antonio Prestes, of which only three or four copies are known. The purchase was made with a view to enriching King Manuel's collection of early Portuguese books and, together with other items, was sent by sea in four massive trunks to London.

Unfortunately, the cases arrived at Southampton in the middle of the famous General Strike of 1926, when all the dockers had left their work and ships' cargoes were dealt with by university students and other helpers. Instead of four trunks arriving, only three reached the customs in London, and King Manuel, who was informed of the loss of what were to be his greatest treasures, was deeply disturbed.

As the four cases were completely covered by insurance with Lloyd's, a firm of assessors placed an advertisement in the personal columns of *The Times* offering a large reward for information leading to the recovery of the missing box. A few days later, the assessors received an anonymous letter from Southampton asking that the reward be raised to £100 and for the publication of the sum to be advertised in the *Daily Telegraph*. This was done, and in the usual mysterious ways adopted by assessors, the contents of box number four in its entirety were handed over at a low public house in the neighborhood of Southampton, to the ex-detective-sergeant in the employ of the assessors; not a volume of the literary treasures was missing. However, the thieves had managed to get rid of the trunk in which the books had been so carefully packed, presumably to avoid discovery.

In the following year, on my next visit to Lisbon, I was urged to purchase the remaining part of the library, which lay in enormous piles in a small house in a side street off Lisbon's leading business thoroughfare. The house was to be cleared and sold by the late owner's heirs, and although it was impossible for me to inspect the books it was obvious that they represented a remarkable collection of Portuguese literature and history, and I succeeded in buying the books for the Library of Congress, Washington, D.C., in 1927. They were packed in huge cases by Thomas Cook and Son—I think some 120—and now form the nucleus of the Portuguese section of the Library of Congress.

In a very interesting volume entitled *Portuguese Essays* (published in 1963) and containing various products of his research as visiting professor of Portuguese studies at New York University, Professor Américo da Costa Ramalho devotes pages 85 to 96 of his work to "Portuguese Publications in the Library of Congress," describing part of this collection, which was still uncatalogued when he saw it.

Senhor Antonio de Carvalho Monteiro was not only a bibliophile but also a devout admirer of Wagner, at least as regards the *Nibelung* operas. On a beautiful plot of ground in Cintra he had a house built to his design. In its dining room the Rhine daughters and other personages of the operas came out of the walls and windows, to greet the guests— at least, their life-size figures in stone appeared to do so, because they were embodied in the doors and walls of this extraordinary chamber. Quite near the house there was a really beautiful building, a large chapel, built entirely of Italian marble to the owner's order.

The most remarkable thing, however, about this country home was the following: In the garden, a short distance from the house and chapel, on the top of a slight hill, appeared the mouth of a well, surrounded by a very low wall. At a touch the wall opened and the visitor went down into the well (which was dry) by a long series of steps. At the bottom he was again met by a blank wall, which opened when touched at the right spot. Through the opening was then visible a series of underground caves, through which ran tiny rivulets. A few minutes' walk led one then to an exit quite near the house. There were goldfish in the rivulets, and the underground caves were lighted up by tiny multi-colored electric lights.

The owner must have spent a fabulous sum on the creation of this unique folly. The whole contraption—house, chapel and gardens—was offered to Mr.

Hearst, but as the house itself was not big enough to contain Mr. Hearst and his guests, the property remained vacant for many years.

In 1924, at intervals of two months or so, I used to find on my desk in London a closely written, rather illegible postcard in which I was urged to visit the sender, who wrote from Toulouse, for the purpose of buying some old French books. The man was unknown to me, and he gave no details; when asked to do so, he sent no list, but only mentioned the names of a few writers of the Renaissance. At last, in order to stop the continuous flow of illegible postcards, I agreed to meet him in Paris on my way to Spain.

After a very severe November Channel crossing from Dover to Calais, when my only thought was to get to bed, I found two men waiting for me at the Paris Hotel; they said they came from Toulouse, one of them being a Monsieur Blanchemain. I received them in my bedroom, and they dragged in several extraordinary antique trunks covered with hide on which the hair was still standing. Although I still felt very unwell and longed to go to bed, I agreed to look at the books, singly, and to put on one side those which might possibly interest me. The first few shown were chiefly fragmentary Books of Hours in appalling condition, but very soon the most fantastic early-sixteenth-century French literature began to appear, and within ten minutes my bed was covered with several dozen first editions of

Ronsard, some in early bindings and one, which was famous for having been burned by the public executioner, *Le Livre des Folastries,* in an exquisite contemporary mosaic binding. There were so many Ronsards that I could hardly believe my eyes. We soon agreed on a price, and I left the books in Paris with an agent and went off to Spain the next morning after promising to visit my new acquaintance in Toulouse, where, he told me, he had many more rare books. On my return from Portugal I stopped at Toulouse and to my amazement found an enormous library containing many more fine early French books.

During my stay at his country house, Monsieur Blanchemain told me the story of the library. He was the grandson of Prosper Blanchemain, who in the 1850's and 1860's was the librarian of the French Ministry of the Interior, the founder of several societies of bibliophiles, including that of the Bibliophiles of Normandy, and a specialist in French sixteenth-century literature.

Prosper Blanchemain had collected every available edition and variant of Ronsard's complete works and of his separate editions, and he had published what, till a few years ago, was considered to be the authoritative edition of this prince of French poets. In 1871, when the Germans invaded France, Prosper Blanchemain was an old man living with his beloved books in a small country house. Knowing the German propensity for loot, and fearing for his treasured books, he had a cavity made in the brick wall of his library, and there he hid most of his Ronsards; he covered this space with wood, painted the same color as the walls, and replaced his bookshelves against the wall as before. Prosper Blanchemain died in 1874, without revealing his secret to his son, who had come to live in this house. The son was on bad terms with his family and did not receive them in this country house. On his father's death in 1924, the Monsieur Blanchemain whom I knew, the grandson of the original collector, arranged with his brothers and sisters to take over the library as part of his share of the father's estate. One day, while standing on a library stepladder, looking at some books, he slipped and desperately clutched at the wall to regain his balance. When he got down off the stepladder, he found to his surprise that the brick wall had left a wooden splinter in his hand. Being of an inquiring turn of mind, he climbed the stepladder again and tapped the wall until he found a spot which sounded hollow, and there was a wooden cover, which he prized open. Thus he discovered the hidden Ronsards! This collection of Ronsards, which was almost complete, became the subject of a monograph by Seymour de Ricci and was displayed in 1925 at the Paris exhibition (mentioned earlier in this chapter) of Ronsard first editions.

Based on this collection and on other copies of Ronsard to be found in public libraries in France and elsewhere, a complete bibliography of Ronsard was projected by the late Alfred Péreire with the help of Mademoiselle Suzanne Brunet, whose knowledge of French sixteenth-century literature and of the rules of bibliography marked her as the most fitting person to carry out this complicated task. Unfortunately, the work is still in the manuscript stage, as Mademoiselle Brunet until recently was fully employed with her daily work as an official of the Réserve at the Bibliothèque Nationale in Paris.

Monsieur Alfred Péreire was himself a great collector and amassed a number of extremely fine French books in what he called "La Bibliothèque d'un Humaniste." In the magnificent mansion which he had inherited from his father and uncle, the millionaire Péreires (who was devotees of Saint-Simonism), he had arranged a number of rooms to contain his library and a private oratory.

The Péreires were descendants of the famous Jacob Rodrigue Péreire (originally Pereira), who in the late eighteenth century devoted himself to the rehabilitation of the deaf-mute. In his youth he fell in love with a young girl who had been mute from birth, and he thereafter sought to develop a method of visual communication for deaf-mutes. One of his inventions was a system of one-hand signals denoting the letters of the alphabet. Although born in Spain (in 1715), he lived most of his life in Paris, where he died (in 1780). He was made a member of the Royal Society of London in 1759.

The Péreires were extremely wealthy; they were the capitalists behind the building of the Spanish Railways and the founders of one of the big Spanish insurance companies. Alfred Péreire himself was greatly interested in literature and full of schemes, not many of which were ever brought to fruition. I remember his coming to me with the idea of publishing *The Times Literary Supplement* in a French translation or establishing a similar publication in French. He got into touch with Mr. Stanley Morison of *The Times* and invited him to Paris to meet a number of editors and publishers of Parisian journals, to discuss the matter. He arranged a great reception and banquet with the choicest wines, and the banquet took place as planned, but unfortunately Mr. Morison did not appear—Monsieur Péreire had entirely forgotten to inform him as to the date of the banquet!

Another curious episode in Monsieur Péreire's literary career was his biography of Pope Pius X; it was printed during the Pope's serious illness and was to be put on sale immediately after the Pope's death. Fortunately for the Pope, he recovered; but Monsieur Péreire had written of him in his biography as "the late Pope"! Other of Monsieur Péreire's grandiose literary schemes resulted in volumes beautifully bound in large quarto and consisting of blank sheets of paper, with only a title and no text.

Paris used to be a happy hunting ground for autographs—the French have always been keen collectors and preservers of written material—and one of the famous old French collectors of autographs was Feuillet de Conches (1798–1887). Some twenty or thirty years ago an old leather case which had been used by him for his autographs was sold to a French dealer with two Spanish documents inside. These documents were entirely in the autograph of Cervantes and dealt with the grain collections in Andalusia, where he was acting as an ill-paid official. They had been published in France at the beginning of the nineteenth century. They are now in the Rosenbach Collection in Philadelphia.

Feuillet de Conches as a collector should not be confused with Philarète de Chasles (1798–1873), the great mathematician and member of the French Academy who has become famous by being the victim of that extraordinary forger Vrain-Lucas who over many years sold him autograph letters of Archimedes, to help him prove certain mathematical theories, and of Cleopatra, Julius Caesar, and Lazarus (after his return from the grave)—all of course written in the best French!

Once I was fortunate enough to obtain two original autograph letters of Saint Francis Xavier; they were written from Goa and reported to the King of Portugal on conditions of life in Japan. The most curious find of that kind, in my recollection, was one that came to light when I removed some slips of old paper which had been used as bookmarks in a Portuguese book. On examination, one folded-up piece of paper turned out to be a letter dated and written from Piratininga (the native name of São Paulo in Brazil), and the writer, who had not forgotten to sign his name, was Father Anchieta, the "Apostle of Brazil."

Among the bibliophiles I met in Paris before the

First World War was the author Pierre Louÿs, who was then married to the youngest daughter of José María de Heredia, the poet (1842–1905), who himself was a remarkable writer. His fame derived chiefly from the sonnets of *Les Trophées,* published in 1893, a year before he was elected a member of the French Academy. In 1901 he became keeper of the splendid Bibliothèque de l'Arsenal, the second-finest national library in Paris.

Pierre Louÿs (he was born Pierre Louis) was favored by nature with a remarkable brain and a special feeling for style, as well as a very handsome figure. In 1894, when he was only twenty-four years of age, he published *Les Chansons de Bilitis,* which is described in the *Oxford Companion to French Literature* as "a so-called translation from the Greek of a poetess contemporary with Sappho which was one of the most successful literary hoaxes of the nineteenth century and which deceived even scholars." With André Gide, Henri de Régnier and Paul Valéry, all three greater men than he, he was successful in founding two important literary reviews, *La Conque* (1891) and *Le Centaure* (1896). He made a great reputation in France with *Aphrodite, moeurs antiques* (1896), which has been called "a novel of courtesan life in ancient Alexandria, a graceful mixture of licentiousness and erudition." He later provoked French society by his rather scandalous publications, including *La Femme et le pantin* (1898) and *Les Aventures du Roi Pausole* (1900). After his death a volume of poems attracted much attention and challenged comparison with some of Baudelaire's verses.

Among his treasures was one that I have been unable to trace—a holograph horoscope bound in contemporary silver fabric written by the astrologer Nostradamus for Queen Catherine de Médicis. This, as far as I know, remains unpublished and has never appeared in any of the various sales which took place from time to time of Pierre Louÿs's collections.

Among the remarkable items shown me by Pierre Louÿs was a cipher manuscript diary adorned with some illustrations and photographs. The cipher was exceedingly difficult, but Pierre Louÿs had managed to find the key. He told me that the contents were extraordinary; the writer was an architect who had included in his manuscript a full account of his love affairs and of all the scandal of the period.

According to Walter Hart Blumenthal, in *Manuscripts*, Volume 14, No. 1 (Winter 1962), the writer, Henri Legrand, born in 1814, began his diary in 1835 and continued his painstaking work for thirty years. In that period he married the natural daughter of the Earl of Clarendon.

The material is authentic and bore notably on the secret history of the period. According to Pierre Louÿs it was unfortunate that the nature of Legrand's revelations, not only about himself but also about the aristocracy of the time, rendered publication impossible. He himself would have been only too delighted if the public taste of his period and of his publishers would have allowed him to edit the diary.

When Pierre Louÿs showed me his books he was a handsome young man, immaculately dressed, living in a beautiful house with a beautiful wife (the daughter of Heredia, whom he was to traduce so grossly in a privately printed work). Pierre Louÿs's reputation and surroundings at that time (the early 1900's) were in terrible contrast to his melancholy and degenerate end which came in 1925, when he, at age fifty-five, was mentally and physically a pitiable wreck.

At the beginning of the Second World War his former secretary, who had married Pierre Louÿs's second wife, came to me with a volume of this diary about which I had not thought for some eighteen years. He also produced Pierre Louÿs's master key to the cipher and expressed the wish to sell the entire manuscript, which comprised many volumes.

I remembered what Pierre Louÿs had told me about the contents. I recalled also that the Danish Ambassador Tage Bull had tried to form a special society of subscribers to underwrite a privately printed edition of the work once it was transcribed —an immense task. He was unsuccessful in his efforts, and the matter lay fallow till Pierre Louÿs's secretary brought me the manuscript. Now the climate of public opinion had changed, even in Paris, and I was able to introduce in April 1940 the then owner of the manuscript and the matter itself to Monsieur Gallimard, of the *Nouvelle Revue française,* who entertained the idea of publishing large extracts from the manuscript in his *Revue* and later publishing the whole diary. However, just before the Fall of Paris I managed to escape and heard nothing more of the negotiations, which presumably came to nothing, as I have not heard of any such publication.

I still think the manuscript, if published, would cause so much trouble that the children or grandchildren of the people whose affairs were so vividly described would bring legal actions against the publishers.

When I was an infant in Paris, Passy was still "the country" for Parisians, and my parents used to occupy the first floor in a house there during the summer months. The occupant of the ground floor was Mademoiselle Hortense Schneider, famous for her rendering of the title role in *La Belle Hélène;* she, to my mother's annoyance, used to kiss me when she saw me in my perambulator. I was reminded of this when I read recently in a French newspaper about the reopening of her house in the Avenue de Versailles, Paris, for a champagne party celebrating the publication of a book, *Offenbach, roi du Second Empire,* by Alain Decaux. The house, which had remained closed for thirty years, in accordance with a clause in her will, is still furnished as it was in the days of her triumphs in Offenbach's operettas. Among her more illustrious visitors were the Tsar,

the Khedive Ismail Pasha of Egypt, the Grand Duke
Constantine of Russia, the King of Greece, Leopold
II of Belgium and the Prince of Wales. *For Kings
Only,* by Curt Siodmak, was based on the life of the
fabulous soubrette who was Jacques Offenbach's
leading lady.

One of the leading lights in the book world before the First World War, and thereafter until 1939,
was Seymour de Ricci, whom I first met through a
fellow undergraduate who was doing Coptic at Oxford. My friend had made the acquaintance of de
Ricci because the latter was also interested in Coptic,
one of many subjects in which he showed his genius.
My friend, E. O. Winstedt, had achieved fame in his
second term at Oxford by finding an unknown and
very obscene series of verses which had been lost in
Juvenal's sixth satire, when he called by chance for a
manuscript at the Bodleian to compare with the
printed text. He later became the secretary of the
Gypsy Society and an official of the Bodleian Library,
where he specialized in Oriental books and manuscripts. His only form of holiday was to go to the
Derby and meet the gypsies, to whom he spoke in
Romany. He was a very shy and reserved savant and
lived a very lonely life.

De Ricci was just the opposite; a tall handsome
man of means, he shone in every society. He had an
extraordinary knowledge of art in every shape and
form, and a unique card-index mind. I shall never
forget how once, at Mr. Henry Yates Thompson's
house in London, after looking only at the outside

of an early Greek incunable, he was able to tell not only the eighteenth- and nineteenth-century auction sales in England in which it had figured, but also the prices it had fetched and the names of the purchasers. Once, when I had shown him a folio Ronsard, he said without opening it, "This copy must have come from Scotland"—and as usual he was right!

De Ricci's published works are numerous, but he was unable to use his wonderful notes on bibliographical matters to the full. He died in the early part of the second World War. He had earlier presented his remarkable collection of fifteen hundred mostly unpublished Voltaire letters, and at his death bequeathed his very remarkable bibliographical material, to the Bibliothèque Nationale, Paris.

During his lifetime he had been retained at a yearly salary by a number of booksellers and bibliophiles, such as Charles W. Clark, Dr. Abraham S. W. Rosenbach, and several London booksellers, to provide bibliographical information when called upon and to help his employers to obtain collections of rare books and manuscripts as they came on the market. It was in consequence of this retaining fee that the famous collection of eighteenth-century books with original drawings which belonged to the Comte Chandon de Briailles was purchased by Dr. Rosenbach. De Ricci was equally brilliant in French and English. It is a pity that such a man with such vast knowledge should ever have to die.

Chapter IX

In the autumn of 1934 rumors began to circulate in London that upwards of three hundred unpublished autograph letters of the Emperor Napoleon I to his Empress Marie-Louise were coming on the market. This was confirmed in November of that year by the publication by Sotheby and Company of an illustrated auction catalogue with eight plates of facsimiles, listing 134 lots comprising a total of 318 autograph letters of Napoleon written from 1810 to March 22, 1814.

This collection included letters written before the betrothal and marriage (February–March 1810), during the tour in the north (May 1810), on the expedition to Russia (May 29–December 12, 1812), during the war in Germany (April 15–November 7, 1813), in the campaign in France (February 2–March 31, 1814), and after the Fall of Paris (April 2–August 24, 1814)—together with a few letters to the Empress from the Emperor's relatives.

Steps were taken by me to bring this extraordinary event to the notice of the French authorities. At a special meeting of the French Academy attended by Messieurs Louis Madelin and Victor Aubry, by Monsieur Picard, Treasurer of the Academy, by Monsieur Réné Doumic, Perpetual Secretary of the Academy, and by myself, after Monsieur Picard had stated that although the Academy had funds at its disposal it had none available for the purchase of these letters, Monsieur Doumic hesitantly suggested that the then premier—"I think," he said, "his name is Monsieur P. E. Flandin"—should be approached. This was unsuccessful. It was necessary for me to approach Monsieur Édouard Herriot, who was then a cabinet member, and he, although ill in bed with a severe attack of influenza, was generous enough to receive me and to insist that the purchase be undertaken. He asked me to try to purchase the letters (through Messrs. Sotheby, of course) before the scheduled date of the sale (Monday, December 17, 1934), from their owner, the Prince of Montenuovo, for the reserve price of £7,500 (which Sotheby's had mentioned confidentially) and the bestowal of the Legion of Honor on the Prince. I transmitted this offer to Messrs. Sotheby, but they were unable to reach the Prince in time, as he was traveling to his several estates in Hungary and Austria.

The sale took place on December 17, 1934, and the letters were purchased on behalf of the French government and brought to Paris. They were met at the Gare du Nord by Monsieur L. Maurice Lang of the *Gazette de l'Hôtel Drouot,* the head of the railway police and myself, and they were duly escorted to the Hotel Louvois, opposite the National Library.

On the following day Pathé News made two documentaries, one in English and the other in French, on the Napoleon letters, with a short explanation of their importance by myself. Thereupon they were handed over to Monsieur Julien Cain at the National Library.

Together with the autograph letters several offers were delivered from press agencies offering for the rights of publication and syndication in the world's press (with the exception of France) more than the £7,500 which the French government had to pay for the letters. One offer was accepted and in March 1935, after the public exhibition of the letters, the Bibliothèque Nationale published them for the first time in full, with an introduction by Monsieur Louis Madelin, in a volume of more than three hundred pages (*Lettres inédites de Napoléon Premier à Marie-Louise, écrites de 1810 à 1814*) and in four different editions, priced from 25 to 150 francs. These letters have subsequently been translated into most European languages and published in many countries.

As pointed out by M. Julien Cain in his introduction to the catalogue of the exhibition at the Bibliothèque Nationale, the special interest of these letters was that although more than 25,000 letters of Napoleon are known to exist and have been published, very few are autograph letters; most were dictated to secretaries. They are for the most part official documents rather than intimate letters. It is not only the rarity of these autograph letters which makes them so interesting, but also the fact that they form a totality from the days of the Austrian marriage to Napoleon's exile on the Island of Elba.

Already Frédéric Masson, the greatest authority on Napoleon's domestic life, commented sadly, in the introduction to his account of Marie-Louise, on the lack of an essential element for the solution of the problem of her relations with the Emperor, that is the letters which they exchanged: he knew of but one letter from her and six or seven from him. This fact is especially noted in the preface to Messrs. Sotheby's catalogue; I will just quote another section of that preface:

"One question cannot surely fail to present itself to anybody who examines the facsimiles in the illustrated catalogues—How did Marie Louise read them? The answer appears to be that, unaided, she did not and could not."

Masson remarks that the Duchesse de Montebello (widow of Marshal Lannes) owed her ascendancy over the Empress partly to her ability to decipher them, and during the campaign in France, Napoleon's brother Joseph was occasionally called in to help. Invaluable as it was, the letter written from Bar-sur-Aube on March 22, 1814, which was intercepted by the Cossacks and forwarded by Blücher to the Empress with a polite note after he had gathered from it important military information, must have been slightly irritating to the intelligence officers on the Prussian Staff.

Perhaps I should explain that the Prince de Montenuovo obtained these letters by inheritance, as he was a descendant of Marie-Louise's second husband Neipperg.

Although from the preceding chapters I seem to have traveled chiefly in Spain and Portugal, this was not the case. I remember once spending some ten days in Tangiers and in Tetuan and Xauen in Spanish Morocco and finding on my return to the Hotel Ritz, Madrid, a telegram asking me to leave immediately for Danzig, whence I was to visit Pelplin, in Poland, to start negotiations about the purchase of the two-volume Gutenberg Bible in contemporary binding which the Polish archbishop of that town was considering selling. Nothing came of the affair; the book was in very poor condition and needed some hundreds of pounds' worth of repairs before being fit to put on the shelves of any library. Subsequently, at the beginning of the Second World War, it was removed by Polish patriots and taken for safety to Canada, where it remained for many years until it was restored by the Canadian government, after long negotiations, to the government of Poland.

On another occasion I was somewhere in Spain, when I received a telegram asking me to proceed immediately to Vienna. This was the story of that sudden move:

About 1930 I had visited Vienna in connection with the sale of the library bequeathed by Don Jaime of Bourbon, son of Don Carlos, the Carlist pretender to the throne of Spain. Don Jaime had lived partly in Paris and partly at his Austrian castle (Schloss Frohsdorf) near the industrial town of Wiener Neustadt, not far from the Hungarian border. In this castle the Comte de Chambord, claimant to the throne of France as Henri V, died in 1883, after having passed the greater part of his life quietly with his royal court and Neapolitan queen, far away from the distractions of lively Vienna. By his will, Don Jaime, who had succeeded to the possessions of Henri V, left Schloss Frohsdorf, its contents and surrounding estate, to his sister Princess Massimo, who was separated from her Italian husband.

The inheritance proved a very difficult one for the unfortunate Princess. First of all, Don Jaime's other sister, the Archduchess d'Este, put in a claim and, immediately after, the two natural sons of another sister, who had died, put in their claim. Not only was the Princess involved in these family lawsuits, but a Hungarian moneylender who had occasionally helped Don Jaime to pay his debts also put in a claim on the estate. He had succeeded in obtaining a sale by auction on the premises of the contents of the wine cellar, and by buying off the few dealers who came from Vienna to attend the sale, he obtained the whole of the contents of the cellar at the price of one krone a bottle! Not content with this, he arranged for the library (also inherited from the Comte de Chambord) to be put under legal sequestration, and the doors which gave access to the library were closed and sealed by the law court of Weiner

Neustadt. For my visit the court bailiff was sent for and the seals were temporarily removed, so that I could enter the library and examine the books. Immediately after I left the room the doors were again locked and the seal replaced.

On the whole, the books were not of excessive rarity, but three items called for special attention. The first was a book by the Abbé Galiani on the importance of wheat for France; it was bound in Sèvres china panels, with a red morocco spine, with the arms of Louis XVI in gold on the sides. The book, enclosed in a contemporary red morocco case, was in perfect condition in this extraordinary binding. It need hardly be said that books in Sèvres bindings are as rare as hens' teeth! The second important item was a volume containing the detailed plans of the interiors of the royal palace of Marly (which is no longer in existence) showing every corner of the building, including the secret staircases and every recess. The volume was made for the Comte de Poisson, brother of the Marquise de Pompadour, and was bound in green morocco with the Comte's coat of arms on the sides. The third item was much more modern. It was a large album containing beautifully executed lifelike colored portraits of the royal personages and their court at Vienna in about 1870 by the then Austrian court painter Goebel. At a later date, after I had been able to purchase the collection and had placed the most remarkable items on exhibition in London, the late Queen Mary came to see the books. She was particularly interested in the album of portraits and was able to identify a number of the archduchesses, whom she had known as a child. Her memory struck me as most remarkable.

I made an offer for the library and left for England. The lawsuits between the heiresses went on, as stated above, till I received a telegram from Vienna informing me that an amicable agreement had been reached by the two sisters, the nephews' case had been dismissed, and my offer was now acceptable, so that with the money received the Hungarian money-lender might be paid off, the embargo lifted, and the Princess' troubles ended.

On arriving at Schloss Frohsdorf, where I met my packer, large wooden cases were ordered to contain the books, when, in the middle of the packing, the Hungarian obtained, I don't know by what means, another court order sequestrating the library. Payment of Don Jaime's debts to the moneylender had already been made by me to the court, but he had declared himself not satisfied, and when the case came before the judge, who was attired in leather shorts and was occupied in smoking a long local pipe with a porcelain bowl, the moneylender claimed not only the money legally due to him, but also the entire library! The rather dim judge unfortunately did not see his way clear to dismiss the Hungarian's suit, but adjourned the case for further consideration. Armed with a typewriter, my lawyer, who was at the same time the legal adviser of the French Embassy in Vienna and of the Princess Massimo, set to work immediately in a shed outside the court, to type a petition claiming the books. He pointed out that the usurer, if I may call him so, could not very well have both the money and the books, and that it was not fair to me that, having paid the money, I should get nothing for it. Rumors of this strange case filtered through the law courts building, and the Court of Appeal, which had its seat in the upper story, let us know, through a messenger, that if the judge on the ground floor decided against us, we should at once appeal to them and they would give their verdict in our favor. Fortunately, when the court reassembled the week after, the judge denied the Hungarian's application on the grounds that he could not very well have both the money and the books!

The packing continued, and the cases were sent off by train; but the Hungarian was not yet satisfied. He denounced the Princess in a letter to the Austrian Inspectorate of Art and Literary Treasures stating that she was smuggling valuable property out of the country. The train was stopped by order of the Inspectorate and the car was taken off before the train was allowed to continue on its journey. A letter to the Inspectorate, however, soon proved that the Hungarian's denunciation was ill-founded as the whole of the goods at Frohsdorf were foreign, that is to say French property, and had never been Austrian. The car was then coupled to another train and in due course left Austria for Hamburg to arrive eventually in London.

Among the relics of the French monarchy to which the Comte de Chambord was heir and which were still at Frohsdorf at the time of my visit, were a pair of shoes of Marie Antoinette and the original bronze head of the statue of Henri IV, which had stood on the Pont-Neuf in Paris until it was thrown into the River Seine at the time of the French Revolution.

After a short exhibition in London, the Chambord relics were taken to Paris for exhibition. The Princess Massimo was kind enough to lend me from Schloss Frohsdorf a very beautiful marble statue of the Comte de Chambord as a young man; and to my surprise we were also lent the original silk *drapeau blanc* which had been made by the women of France for the Comte de Chambord when he was to go to France as King, after the Franco-German War. There were, too, some other very interesting relics of the Bourbons still in the hands of the French nobility.

Even larger crowds came to see these relics and the library than had come to the exhibition of King Manuel's books. One day I had the pleasure of greeting the last secretary of the Comte de Chambord; he had lived at Schloss Frohsdorf and now, a very old man, was happy to see again some of the books he had seen there before the Comte's death in 1883. He told me many interesting stories of the court and of the visits paid to the King-in-exile by his loyal followers from France.

One morning in Paris a very tall aristocratic-looking old lady came to see the exhibition and, after going round the showcases, told me, *"Moi, j'ai un merveilleux souvenir de Sa Majesté."* I thought she would like to be asked to lend it for the exhibition, and I suggested that she might like to do so, whereupon she said, *"Impossible, Monsieur, tout à fait impossible."* Thinking that she wanted to be pressed even more, I again insisted that it would be very generous of her to lend this souvenir for the exhibition, even for the short time that it would still be open. She again said, *"Impossible."* My curiosity being aroused, I asked her point-blank what the souvenir was. *"Un baiser, Monsieur, de Sa Majesté,"* was the answer!

She then explained to me that it was the custom among the French nobility on their honeymoon, to go to Frohsdorf to present the new bride to the King, as at court, and that he would then bestow a chaste kiss on her forehead—and this was what had happened to my visitor.

During the course of the exhibition there was a great rush on the part of the French nobility to secure from the King's library, presentation copies which had been given to the King by their ancestors.

Another very successful exhibition held in Paris was visited by most of the bibliophiles—that of the magnificent collection of books and manuscripts of Baudelaire, Verlaine and Rimbaud, which I had been able to buy from Edward J. Titus, the first husband of Helena Rubinstein (the Queen of Cosmetics, who died in April 1965, aged ninety-four). Mr. Titus, who had met Helena Rubinstein in Australia and had, to judge from some of the books still in his library at Cagnes-sur-Mer, supplied his wife with prescriptions for beauty preparations, had settled in Paris at the end of the First World War and had acted as publisher for some contemporary writers. He had tired of Paris and settled in a beautiful house on the hilltop at Cagnes-sur-Mer and devoted himself to his books.

He suddenly made up his mind to clear out his collection of the modernist French poets, and I took the opportunity of having a catalogue made and exhibiting the books in Paris. I was greatly helped by the Paris Prefect of Police, who very kindly lent for the exhibition the original pistol with which Rimbaud had attacked Verlaine in Brussels and the daily police reports on Verlaine, who was continuously followed by detectives; these almost invariably recorded the poet's returning drunk from his favorite café.

Shortly after my return to France I planned a round of visits to private libraries in the French Châteaux with a view to inducing their owners to dispose of unwanted books which might be of great interest to bibliophiles. Before starting on this systematically and organizing a series of tours to each French province in turn, I arranged with a friend to make a trial trip to Normandy.

After an exchange of correspondence we were welcomed in a small manor, to which the appellation *château* could hardly be applied, and were shown to the attics, where in two small rooms there were a number of dust-covered books stored on primitive shelves. We rummaged through the books and, in addition to a few unimportant items, discovered an early folio atlas in a magnificent gilt binding which was entirely tarnished by age and dirt. After restoration in Paris by the house of Léon Gruel, it turned out to be a wonderful specimen of French binding. It is now one of the treasures in the finest private collection of bindings in England, that of Major J. R. Abbey, of Redlynch House, Redlynch, near Salisbury.

The most interesting thing about this visit, however, was not the presence of this fine item in the attic, but the presence of many thousands of sleeping flies which had congregated to pass the winter and await the coming of the warm days of summer. It was an answer to that well-known facetious question, "Where do the flies go in the wintertime?" Obviously to the undisturbed attics of Normandy!

At the beginning of the Second World War I was still in Paris, where the Paris book trade seemed to be stricken with paralysis. About Christmas 1939 I was approached by a French architect and decorator who had been charged with the refurnishing and redecorating of the Paris offices of Renault. He wished to make one of the walls of the director's offices a blaze of color and for that purpose wanted to put up bookshelves filled with fine eighteenth-century books with decorative gilt backs in various shades of morocco. There were plenty of such volumes in stock at that time, and Messrs. Renault paid a very large sum to have their wall displaying just those shades of color which were required to make them more impressive. At that time, in England things were very different.

As soon as 1940 began, there was much more movement in the Paris book trade, and the French millionaires started buying again at high prices. I was offered then, by a member of a Spanish noble family, a number of books which he had inherited from his father's library. Among them was a book which I was unable to buy but which I have deeply regretted ever since. It was a perfect copy of the first edition of the very rare comedies of Cervantes, bound in contemporary red morocco. At a later date I tried to find out what had happened to the book, but I never was able to trace it again.

I was all the more sorry not to have been able to deal with this item, as many years previously I had been successful in obtaining a copy of the first edition of the second part of *Don Quixote* equally bound in old red morocco. This volume joined the famous, almost complete collection of *Don Quixote* which had been formed by the famous former Mayor of Buenos Aires, Señor Pueyredon, which is presumably still in the possession of his family. Señor Pueyredon, who played a leading part in Argentine society, resigned with the advent of Perón as President.

A curious episode during the early months of 1940 was my only deal with the late King Farouk of Egypt. A Parisian bibliophile came to me with a remarkable manuscript. This comprised, in several morocco-bound volumes, Napoleon's private list of his high officers; the Emperor used to have it on his desk, and he would consult it whenever the question of promotion for one of his army officers came up. This was, of course, a first-class Napoleonic item for a collector.

It was well known among bibliophiles that King Farouk was enamored of Napoleonic relics. He was also known to have a large fortune and to be able to buy items of great value. As there was some uncertainty as to letters from Paris reaching Egypt in the ordinary way, I arranged for my offer of this choice item to be taken to Fakri Pasha, the Egyptian ambassador in Paris, who was a brother-in-law of King Farouk. I also arranged to show Fakri Pasha the set of books in question. He was charmed by these and assured me that the letter would be sent to Egypt in the diplomatic pouch.

Soon after, an order to buy the books came from Egypt on behalf of the King, and I thereupon bought the item from the owner. The books were taken to the Egyptian Embassy and sent to the King. What was my astonishment, however, to get shortly afterward a letter from the King's secretary making an offer for these items of about a quarter of the price which had been asked!

I immediately went to see Fakri Pasha and asked for an explanation, in view of the fact that the King had definitely ordered this item at the price mentioned. The Ambassador replied that "in the Orient an order to buy does not mean what it does in the West" and tried to excuse the King's proceedings in this manner. I at once asked to have the items returned and put an end to this very unpleasant experience with a ruler of Egypt.

Among the interesting men with whom I had to deal between the two wars, was that great actor Sacha Guitry. He used to call, at first, with Lucien Guitry, his father, and Yvonne Printemps, to whom he was then married. The three of them acted as dramatically in their private lives as on the stage, and they would strike attitudes the memory of which would remain with one all one's life, especially when they were acting with and *at* one another.

Lucien Guitry, wrapped in a large cloak, would address himself to his son on the subject of his love for Shakespeare and his quest for one of the four Shakespeare folios, while Sacha Guitry always remained master of himself, with a full knowledge of what he wanted. Today, I suppose, it would not be wrong to assert that the Sacha Guitry collection of printed books and manuscripts, including first editions of Molière and others, and Marshal Foch's historic Order of the Marne, is probably the best collection in private hands in France.

In addition to early books, Sacha Guitry also collected autographs and original manuscripts of French authors, such as Octave Mirbeau, and would spend very large sums on their acquisition. As he had become rich from the royalties for his plays and from his acting in them, he was, to my knowledge, the only actor who was able to buy practically everything he wanted, either privately or at public auction. Whenever I was in Paris, I always made a point of calling on him, and he invariably invited me to see him perform in whatever play was being presented at the time.

Before the First World War I was occupied with collectors of miniatures—European, Persian and Indian. Among these collectors were such famous men as Dr. Martin, the Swedish diplomat and connoisseur of Oriental carpets; Baron Maurice de Rothschild, son of Baron Edmond de Rothschild and sometime French Senator; the Comte Alexandre de Laborde, Secretary of the Société Française des Réproductions de Manuscrits à Peintures; Monsieur Jean Pozzi, the French diplomat and owner of a magnificent collection of Oriental miniatures and antiquities; Mr. Calouste S. Gulbenkian, who before the First World War was living modestly on the Quai d'Orsay and who already showed his talent for the purchase of beautiful objects (at the time, chiefly Oriental); and last but not least, the Comte Paul Durrieu, member of the Institut and expert connoisseur of French illuminated manuscripts.

On one of my visits to the apartment of Comte Durrieu, who specialized in fifteenth-century miniatures, he showed me part of his beautiful collection of manuscripts. He kept them in a cupboard in his bedroom, each manuscript neatly contained in a shirt box from one of the great Paris stores. While most of the collections in the hands of private owners of that time have been dispersed or are in public possession, such as the Gulbenkian treasures, I believe that the wonderful manuscripts which belonged to Comte Paul Durrieu are still in the possession of his heirs.

It would take too much space to enumerate all the Comte Durrieu's contributions to the history of book illumination, but it is necessary to recall especially his *Les Antiquités judaïques et le peintre Jean Foucquet* (1907–1908) and *Le Boccace de Munique* (Paris and Munich, 1910), and other contributions to the knowledge of Jean Fouquet in a number of French official art publications.

One of the collectors of miniatures was Georges Wildenstein, who was then a young boy, living in his parents' house. He was most eager to buy fine early Italian miniatures, which he used to frame and hang up in his simply furnished student bedroom.

In Paris I had the pleasure of meeting Monsieur Tissandier, the son and nephew of the famous Tissandier brothers, the early specialists in ballooning. I had the privilege of seeing the famous Tissandier collections of ballooning antiques and the Tissandier Aeronautical Library when it was still in his splendid apartment. Monsieur Tissandier decided to move into a more modern and convenient flat and, before doing this, allowed me to buy both the library and the furniture and other aeronautical antiquities collected by his father and uncle, both of whom had spent a lifetime in such collecting. Both the furniture and the library went to the United States, to a collector of aeronautics; the books, I understand, have been transferred to the Library of Congress, in Washington, D.C. Neither of these collections could ever be duplicated.

To accommodate King Manuel's desire for Portuguese books, I began to visit Spain, as well as Portugal, quite regularly, and there I made many friends and clients. Among them was that remarkable man Don José Lázaro y Galdiano (1862–1947), founder of the museum which now bears his name. He was extremely handsome and of neat appearance, with a wonderful beard, which he preserved till the last. He was a friend of Emilia Pardo Bazán, the most famous woman writer of her time in Spain, and advised by her he became the editor of *La España Moderna,* the leading Spanish literary review. Later he married a wealthy Argentine widow and began his collections of art and literature. After various difficulties he soon became an expert in antiques and paintings and amassed in his Madrid home what could be called a Spanish "Wallace Collection" or "Hertford House." He also collected books and manuscripts, and it was in connection with these that I got to know him. The collections were saved during the Spanish Civil War by Dr. A. Rodríguez-Moñino, who, after the war, joined the staff of the museum, which José Lázaro bequeathed to General Franco, and which was opened to the public in 1951.

In the same year, Dr. A. Rodríguez-Moñino published at Valencia in a limited edition of five hundred copies a pamphlet of twenty-six pages, entitled *Don José Lázaro visto por Rubén Darío (1899) y Miguel de Unamuno* (*1909*), with a preliminary note by himself, in which articles by these two illustrious authors are reproduced, together with a large portrait of the subject of the essays.

My first visit to Madrid was on the sixth of December, 1920, for the purpose of visiting the chief Spanish bookseller of the time, who had not had any visitors from abroad during the First World War. He chronicled the event in his diary, which he entitled *Liber Peccatorum,* though he intermingled a little fantasy with his facts. The journey was very fruitful; I was able to buy not only some first-class incunabula, but also some very rare travel books, including the second, third and fourth *Relaciones* of Cortes on the conquest of Mexico. These letters of his to the King of Spain were both beautifully printed and rare. I was always hoping to find one day the first *Relation,* which is known to have appeared in print, the place, printer and date all being known, but no copy of the book has ever come to light.

A few years after my first visit to Madrid, during which time the local booksellers used to send descriptive lists of books they had for sale, a letter came from one of them with the following contents: "A friend of mine has just brought to me the first *Relation* of Cortes. You know how rare this is. If you send me a check immediately for £50 I can get you the book and will send it to you by registered post."

I translated the letter to one of my chiefs and advised him to send the check. I explained that it was like taking a lottery ticket, with a possibility, though perhaps not a probability, of getting the first prize!

The check was sent and I waited expectantly, but nothing arrived. A few months later I was in Madrid and called on this man. I told him that, as the parcel he had sent was registered, inquiries would be made through the London General Post Office to the Spanish authorities and this would lead to all kinds of difficulties. I asked him, first of all, to let me know at what post office he had registered the parcel. He replied that he had not sent the book himself, but that a friend had posted it and in order to avoid going to a post office had simply slipped it into a letter box. I said that further inquiries would still have to be made, and the dealer replied that he did not think any more inquiries should be made, because, he said, "after all, I think my friend really stole the book." I saw that the whole thing was a fraud and told the man that he was to make special lists and that we would recoup the £50 sent to him by ordering books to that amount from him.

We had no further trouble with the man and were able to do business with him to our mutual satisfaction. Some twelve years later he introduced me to a library which was for sale and his behavior on that occasion caused me to remember the earlier trouble we had had with him. I asked him suddenly point-blank, "Tell me the true story of the first *Relation* of Cortes." He replied, "When I wrote to you a long time ago about the first Cortes *Relation* I was in need of money and knew that no one in Spain would trust

me with a peseta. Then I immediately thought of
your firm and wrote to you offering the Cortes and
asking for a fifty-pound check." I then asked him,
"But what did you want the fifty pounds for so
urgently?" And he smilingly replied, "I needed it to
get married on."

On one of my visits to Madrid I acquired one of
the two or three Books of Privileges which Christopher Columbus had written out for his own use
and for the use of his son during his famous lawsuit,
with manuscript notes by himself. At a later date this
went to the Henry Edward Huntington Library in
San Marino, California.

Another episode, which was much less successful
from my point of view, was that of the Veragua
Archives. The Duke of Veragua, well known in Spain
for the breeding of the black bulls which used to
figure in the best bullfights, was short of money and
needed a very large sum to pay his gambling debts.
A friend of mine heard about this and started negotiations for the purchase of the whole of the Duke's
historic Columbus Archives. I went to Madrid and
in the presence of my friend and the Duke checked
the whole of this most important of Spanish archives,
which included the most interesting documents for
the history of Columbus himself, and his relations
with King Ferdinand and Queen Isabella in the
discovery of the Indies. We agreed on a very large
price, some millions of pesetas, and a society was

formed for the purchase of the archives and their transfer to an American institution.*

Since the Duke did not wish to be derided as a descendant of Columbus who had sold his family papers without government consent, and as I, of course, also refused to undertake their purchase without the full approval of the Spanish authorities, the consent of the Council of State was necessary. But, as several of the members were intimate friends of the Duke, there was very little doubt that the consent of the Council would be given. Unfortunately, however, just before the Council was to meet—the Council met only at very rare intervals—King Alfonso XIII called in General Primo de Rivera as dictator, who promptly dismissed the Council.

With this change, the Duke remained laden with the burden of his debts, and so a scheme was devised on his behalf, to provide cardboard medals for subscribers to a fund for the purchase of the archives for the Spanish state. This proved unsuccessful; but, as the date for the opening of the Barcelona and Madrid National Exhibitions was near, it was arranged that funds intended for the exhibitions should be devoted to the purchase of the archives from the Duke, and that these should be exhibited at the Barcelona Exhibition and thereafter handed

* The idea of a society for that purpose was hatched in the fertile brain of Gabriel Wells, the very successful New York dealer who, beginning by peddling subscription sets, ended as a wealthy bookseller to equally wealthy clients.

over for preservation to the Archives of the Indies, at Seville. This was successful; but the sum paid was only about half the sum which we originally offered to the Duke. The Duke unfortunately was killed by the Communists during the Spanish Civil War, and his corpse was left lying by the roadside—a tragic end for the descendant of Christopher Columbus!

Another manuscript of Columbian interest also came my way. It was the earliest extant letter written in, and signed from, America. In this unique original document, Diego Columbus, Christopher Columbus' eldest son, who was born in 1474, describes his life on Hispaniola and the activities of the Spaniards in the new colonies under his rule. It contains a record of the earliest expedition to the Island of Cuba, which was to be colonized by Diego; he had fitted out an expedition of 300 men in 1511, and had sent it out under Diego Velásquez "to see what secrets lay there." Throughout the closely written pages his expressed desire is to aggrandize his sovereign and govern the colony in the interests of the Crown, with humane regard for the interests of the governed.

Diego Columbus' enemies had accused him of wishing to become sovereign of the Indies, but his statement in this letter which he addressed to the famous Cardinal Francisco Ximénez de Cisneros, Archbishop of Toledo, on January 12, 1511, from Santo Domingo—"they [the Indians] have been made to understand that we have only gone amongst them to make Christians of them, that they may serve God and become subjects to His Highness [i.e., King

Ferdinand the Catholic]"—shows eloquently enough how far from his thoughts such an ambition was.

Reporting upon the expedition to Cuba, Diego Columbus writes: "The Island is very large, though they have not yet transversed it all. Now a town has sprung up in the North, to which Diego Velásquez, whom I have mentioned, has given the name of Asunción, through his having arrived there on Ascension Day."

Diego describes some of the vegetation and animals found on the island: There are no trees like those in Castille, but the strawberry tree yields *madroños* in abundance; it is a land where big-game hunting is obtainable, unlike the place where it is obtainable only upon a small scale. In addition to quantities of gold in all the rivers, Columbus says, "Diego Velásquez also writes that a native informed him of the existence of pearls in one part of the island, although he is not certain, as he has not been to the spot himself." He adds that there must be some things on this island which would be of advantage to His Highness (King Ferdinand).

The letter was written by Columbus' secretary and contains the final words, "Illustrious Sir, Servitor of your very Rev. Lordship, whose very magnificent hands are kissed by," in the autograph of Diego Columbus himself and is signed "El Almirante" (the Admiral).

This document, of superlative interest and importance, was later offered for sale in the catalogue entitled *The History of American Documents,* issued by the Rosenbach Company in 1949. In 1929 it was already described in a brochure printed by the Curwen Press in fifty copies. The original was purchased from the Rosenbach Company by the late Thomas B. Gilchrist.

Although various letters exist which were written by Christopher Columbus, those of his son Diego are very much rarer, for, besides this hitherto unrecorded letter, only two other extant personal letters of his are recorded, and but three additional documents which bear his signature. Of the existing letters, however, the one described above is the earliest, and though in the text of it he refers to previous communications, they are entirely unrecorded and presumed to be nonexistent.

Diego had entered the service of Prince Juan, the son of King Ferdinand and Queen Isabella, as a page, and was with him when Christopher Columbus undertook his first voyage to America. After Christopher Columbus' death in 1506, Diego presented himself before the King as his father's proposed successor, making strenuous efforts to wrest from King Ferdinand all the dignities and privileges which he considered due to his family and of which the great admiral had been deprived. These efforts were unavailing in spite of the fact that Diego had been brought up at the court and was popular. When King Ferdinand returned from Naples in 1508, Diego again put forward his claims, but was told that it was impossible to grant a hereditary title or right to so important a commission as that of Admiral of the

Indies without first knowing whether Christopher Columbus' successors were likely to possess the necessary qualifications.

Before this reply was received, Diego had asked permission to make representations to the law courts with a view to confirming the conditions which had been entered into and signed by Ferdinand and Isabella and his father, Christopher. The lawsuit resulted in a favorable verdict for Diego, but the King persisted in evading its fulfillment. It was only after his marriage to María de Toledo, niece of the Duke of Alba, and the King's favorite, that through the influence of his wife's relatives he was appointed Governor—not Viceroy—of the Indies in 1508.

In 1519 Charles I of Spain was elected Holy Roman Emperor (to become Charles V), and when he sailed from Corunna to acquire the imperial crown, Diego Columbus, who was then temporarily in Spain, lent the Emperor the sum of ten thousand ducats to enable him to present himself before his German subjects in a manner befitting his state. In recognition of this loan, Charles V confirmed the title of Viceroy of the Indies, which Diego had often used and which King Ferdinand had persistently withheld.

By a curious coincidence, after the Second World War, two original letters dated 1493 and signed by King Ferdinand and Queen Isabella were brought to me at Oxford for sale. They were both connected with the provisioning of Columbus' second journey to the Indies, with ships' biscuits.

Both these important documents, which were

hitherto unknown and unrecorded, are now in the Casa del Libro in Puerto Rico. They were purchased by the late great connoisseur of printing and civilization, Elmer Adler.

My involvement with Columbus did not end then. Before the Second World War, on a voyage to Spain, I was asked to visit Jerez, to inspect some Columbus documents in the possession of a titled family. My attention had been called to this by a solicitor in that town, and I gladly took the opportunity of visiting the home of the Spanish and only real sherry. The titled family was descended from Columbus, one of the two families which had been passing some centuries in lawsuits against the other female branch of the Columbus family. The documents related to this lengthy and important lawsuit for the privileges granted by Ferdinand and Isabella in the way of customs and other economic rights in Central America. Attached to these seventeenth-century papers was a letter written on paper bearing the names of Ferdinand and Isabella (*Yo el Rey, yo la Reyna*), granting Columbus the privileges claimed. The pin which attached this letter to the documents was ancient and handmade, but the ink, though old, was not fifteenth-century, and the writing seemed to me very doubtful. I was not satisfied with the authenticity of the letter, especially when the writer of the letter made use of the term "West Indies," which was not yet in use at the time the letter was supposed to have been written. I therefore refused to buy the document and dismissed the matter from my mind. The letter was, of course, not genuine; it had been fabricated in the seventeenth century for the use of the lawsuit to uphold the family claims against the Crown. What was my surprise, then, to find last year, in a pamphlet illustrating future treasures to be offered for sale by auction in May by Christie's, the reproduction of the same letter. Although apparently the authorities at the British Museum had no doubt about the genuineness of the document, in consequence of certain representations made to the auctioneers the letter was withdrawn and not offered for sale.

Thereafter it transpired that the letter had been offered for an exhibition in Spain but had naturally been refused by the authorities there, although it had been published in an article in a Jerez newspaper some years after my visit!

Chapter X

The chase after books is one of the most fascinating, and the chase after Americana one of the most exciting, owing to their greater rarity. After 1919 the giant collectors Henry Edward Huntington and Sir Robert Leicester Harmsworth were eager rivals, and there were a number of other millionaires competing with them.

There is a certain Americanum printed in a small Spanish provincial town in the early sixteenth century which contains the first account of the first journey undertaken by a European into the center of what is now the United States of America. For some reason this little quarto is of excessive rarity, the only copies known being one in the New York Public Library and another, imperfect one in the British Museum.

One day in a bibliography I found an account of a third copy of this book, belonging to a private collector in Spain. I naturally thought that if this man possessed this exceptional rarity he would have more books of a similar nature and possibly be willing to sell them. On visiting this man's home, in a rather obscure town, I stayed overnight and was unable to see his library until the next morning. I looked at every book on the shelves, but to my surprise I found very little there with the exception of some modern books on local history, heraldry and genealogy. I was disappointed at having come such a very long way to prospect for this Americanum. I looked in vain and at last asked him outright, "Where is your copy of so and so?" He looked at me with surprise and said, "But how did you know that I had this book?" My heart sank and I asked, "What has happened to it?" He replied that there was a very curious story connected with this book and this is what he told me:

"Forty years ago, when I was a young man, a student friend of mine came to me as he knew I liked books and brought the book you mentioned; he said that I could have it if I gave him fifty pesetas. The book seemed to me interesting and I took it and put it on my shelves after giving him the fifty pesetas he had asked. A few years later, after I had shown the book in Madrid my friend returned and said: 'A dreadful thing has happened. You must give me back that book I sold you, as my father is now missing it from his library.' I returned the book, but he did not give me back my fifty pesetas. That was forty years ago."

On hearing this extraordinary story I felt unhappy and very chilly, as this was winter and the news I had just heard was not of a very cheering nature. However, on hearing that I was very interested in knowing the fate of the book, the man gave me the name and address of his former friend, and I pledged my word that I would never let the friend know where I had obtained his name and address. I was then on the way to Lisbon, as usual for King Manuel, but on my return to the Franco-Spanish border I wrote to the address given me and was able to meet a very charming old gentleman with whom I soon got on very well. When I asked whether he was in possession of a library, he informed me that he had a very small collection of books which he had inherited and that he kept them in a small country house in the Pyrenees. I pressed him to let me see his library and we drove a long way through the mountains to a small village.

On arriving at the house, we found it locked and were unable to get in; he had no keys and his housekeeper was out. By dint of questioning the neighbors we were able to find her in the village, and she opened the front door. But, as it was already four o'clock, the house was very dark. The electric light failed, as it often did in Spain, and when we got to the room which was called the library, it turned out to be nothing more than a small sitting room, with a number of open shelves containing modern books. However, two miniature bookcases seemed to contain a number of older books. More keys were obtained and a candle, and I was given permission to look at the books by candlelight. I went through them rather hastily, as it was getting darker and much colder; I did not know whether the book I was looking for had ever been replaced in the "father's library."

The books were a curious collection, chiefly theological, most of them bearing the name of a sixteenth-century missionary. I picked out a few to look at again, and almost the last book I found on the last shelf was the American rarity. When examined, it proved to be a beautiful uncut copy of the book, in contemporary vellum binding; but when it was collated, one leaf in the middle of the book was found to be missing. I expressed a wish to buy that book and half a dozen others, and I made an offer, which was almost the price of the house. My new friend would not give me an answer at once, but said he would write to me to London. So I returned to England, not knowing if my long and exciting trip had been successful or not. Four days later two small packets arrived, and I was able to send a very large check to the former owner.

Fortunately, it was possible to have a facsimile made of the missing leaf from the British Museum copy. The book is now in a public library devoted to Americana in the United States.

Elsewhere I have spoken of Salvador Babra, the young architect turned bookseller, who first brought Spanish incunabula to the attention of Ludwig Rosenthal in Munich. Subsequently, on my journeys to Spain on behalf of King Manuel, I was able to buy many items of interest from him.

On one occasion Señor Babra produced part of the manuscript Spanish archives of the Duchess of Aveiro—"the father and mother of the Spanish missions," as she was called by one of the numerous missionaries she patronized.

All the letters and reports addressed to her by the missionaries from the outlandish spots at which they were stationed were of the greatest interest and entirely unpublished. The most exciting of these letters, in my opinion, were the letters of Father Eusebio Francisco Kino written on native paper from California on his first visit there.

These letters were catalogued and the entire collection bought by Mrs. Millard, of Pasadena, who sold them to Mr. Henry Edward Huntington. A Jesuit, Father Ernest J. Burrus, is now editing them, and they are now published under the title *Correspondencia del P. E. F. Kino con la Duquesa de Aveiro* in Madrid in the *Colección Chimalista acerca de la Nueva España.*

On one of my visits to Madrid, I was able to inspect King Alfonso XIII's royal library in the palace through the kindness of that genial librarian and author, the Conde de las Naves, who not only explained the curious composition of the library to me, but was most generous in treating me to some of his royal master's excellent wine.

The royal library contained at that time, and still does, some extraordinarily important manuscripts and books on the history of America and of Spain, but, in addition, I was shown shelf after shelf of presentation copies of the ornate and sometimes too elaborate morocco bindings presented by the authors of comparatively unknown works to the King and to his children. The royal librarian explained that on marriage, Spanish infantes and infantas used to withdraw the books presented to them, so that part of the library was in a state of flux. When King Alfonso XIII abdicated the throne and left Spain, I took the opportunity of recalling this fact to the King's secretary and pointed out that each of the King's children was entitled to withdraw such books from the royal library as were his personal property. I do not, however, know if anything ever came of this suggestion.

Chapter XI

Interspersed among my journeys to Portugal and Spain came three long visits to the United States. The first was in the winter of 1925, when I was able to induce Mr. Henry Edward Huntington to add to his library in San Marino important unpublished Spanish manuscripts relating to the rebellion of the Pizarros in Peru. At the same time, Mr. Huntington bought some of the rarest printed Americana I had ever been able to find during my journeys in Spain and Portugal.

The manuscripts about the Pizarros and the rebellion in Peru had lain for a long time in the possession of the widow of a noted Madrid paleographer. I had seen them before, but the widow had at that time been unwilling to sell them. I think she used the money she was paid for them to provide a dowry for her eldest daughter.

A privately printed catalogue entitled *From Panama to Peru, the Conquest of Peru by the Pizarros, the Rebellion of Gonzalo Pizarro and the Pacification of La Gasca (An epitome of the original signed documents to and from the Conquistadores Francisco, Gonzalo, Pedro and Hernando Pizarro, Diego de Almagro, and Pacificator La Gasca, together with the original signed manuscript Royal Decrees*) was issued in 100 copies and is today a very great rarity. Practically all the copies of the catalogue were handed over with the original manuscripts and their transcription to Mr. Huntington in 1926.

The manuscripts included a remarkable letter dated 1550 from Gonzalo Fernández de Oviedo y Valdés, the first historian of the Indies, in which he asked Pedro de la Gasca, the agent of the Spanish Crown, for the latest particulars about the Pizarro rebellion, so that he might include the details in his forthcoming *History of the Indies.* Among the rarest of the letters was one by Francisco Pizarro, the conqueror of Peru; since he was unable to sign his name, he made his mark in the shape of a paraph, which he placed on each side of his name written for him by his secretary.

I had the opportunity for some private chats with Mr. Huntington, and I asked him what was his favorite manuscript in his collection. He at once replied, "The letter [dated July 20, 1819] which Charles Lamb addressed to Frances Kelly, the actress, in which he proposed to her." Mr. Huntington also owned Miss Kelly's reply, written on the same day, refusing Lamb's offer.

On returning to London after this important sale I found that an English picture dealer, on reading in *The Times Literary Supplement* of the Huntington Library's acquisition of the Pizarro papers, offered the firm with which I was then connected the enormous collection of English manuscripts, letters and documents which had formed the archives of the Earls of Huntingdon. This collection was bought, duly catalogued, and in 1926, on my second visit to America, I was able to sell to Mr. Huntington this collection which bore almost the same name as his own—"The Huntingdon Papers (The Archives of the Noble Family of Hastings)."

In the collection there were six separate parts: (1) charters and royal grants with seals, A.D. 1101–1688; (2) historical correspondence from the time of King Henry VIII to the death of Queen Elizabeth, A.D. 1513–1603; (3) historical correspondence during the reign of King James I, A.D. 1603–1625; (4) America— Sir Walter Raleigh, 1597–1618; the Virginia Company, 1610–1625; Florida, 1767–1768; and the War for Independence, 1776; (5) historical correspondence from the time of Charles I to the flight of James II, A.D. 1625–1688; (6) historical correspondence relating to Scotland, the Old and Young Pretenders, and the Rebellions of 1715 and 1745.

The great interest of this collection was that the destinies of the Hastings family, one of the oldest in the British peerage, had been, from the time of William the Conqueror, inextricably linked with that of the ruling monarch, and the collection shows how the family's fortunes varied from reign to reign. The oldest document in the collection bears the date 1101; from that time on, there was no English reign in which a Hastings did not play a part.

A series of letters and documents from 1610 to the

end of the eighteenth century showed what the Hastingses did in the New World, and we find a Captain Edward Hastings, brother of the fifth Earl of Huntingdon, in the company of Sir Walter Raleigh on the famous "Island Voyage." At the same time the Hastingses were helping to colonize Virginia; and later in the eighteenth century they helped to colonize East Florida.

As regards the charters, there is no such remarkable collection of charters and great seals to be found, outside the collection in the British Museum. In fact the state of preservation of this collection is on the whole superior to the seals in the British Museum.

Among the historical correspondence we find a letter of King Henry VIII informing Huntingdon that he is determined to invade France; a letter of Queen Mary appealing for troops to be levied in haste for the relief of Calais. This appeal was made too late; four days later Calais fell to the French. There are numerous letters from Queen Elizabeth, including two of the highest historical importance dealing with Mary Queen of Scots and her captivity, letters from Robert Dudley, Earl of Leicester, including one in which he criticizes the proposed marriage of Queen Elizabeth to the French Duc d'Alençon.

The original documents on the colonization of Virginia (1610–1625) comprise the original circular letter, dated March 10, 1610, sent out by the Virginia Company giving details of the infant colony, as well as three original share certificates, known also as "Bills of Adventure," signed by the secretary and sealed with the Virginia Company's seal.

Before the sale was concluded I received information from London that an additional lot of manuscripts forming part of the same archives had been offered to and purchased by the firm. This important parcel of documents, I was informed, would be thrown in without extra charge. The deal went through and the later manuscripts in London were sent to California also without any charge. On their being examined in London before being sent away, what was the surprise of those responsible for the London end of the deal, to find a manuscript confirmation of a grant of land made by King Henry VIII to Thomas Grey, Marquis of Dorset, dated June 29, 1527. As described by Mr. Herbert C. Schulz, the curator of manuscripts at the Huntington Library, "It is signed at the top by King Henry, while at the bottom, underneath the usual flap of Vellum folded over for attaching the seal, appear the signatures of Sir Thomas More, and Thomas Wolsey, Cardinal of York. Recalling the circumstances that Henry condemned More to the executioner's block eight years later, in 1535, and indirectly brought about the death of Wolsey, who expired on his way to the Tower, in 1530, the document forms a relic of happier days in the lives of this formidable trio of Tudor personalities."

Another letter which was found in the archives was written by John Fletcher, the Elizabethan

dramatist, addressed to the Countess of Huntingdon, who was a cousin of his literary partner, Francis
Beaumont. A very large collection of documents with
the great royal seals in fine condition was included
in the collection.

The Huntington Library, with the purchase of the
Huntingdon-Hastings collection, now holds what is
probably the largest collection of English medieval
documents in any library outside Great Britain.

On my first journey to the United States, which
started in the winter of 1925, I met Mr. Speck, of
New Haven, Connecticut, who was then busily engaged in amassing a magnificent collection of first
editions of German literature of the eighteenth and
early nineteenth centuries as a gift to Yale University. While we were lunching together, Mr. Speck,
who was particularly interested in Goethe, asked me
for my help in tracing a book he had been looking
for for forty years. On being asked what this was, he
told me that after reading an account, in Eckermann's
Table Talk, of the interview between Napoleon and
Goethe, during which Napoleon had questioned
Goethe about Werther, he had tried in vain to find
Napoleon's own copy in French of the *Sorrows of
Werther*. Curiously enough, I was able to give him
some definite information about this very item.

In 1920 a bookseller in a small way in the little
town of Puy-de-Dôme in central France had issued
a catalogue in which he described a French *Werther*,
printed in 1804 in Paris, bound in its original mot-
tled calf, and bearing Napoleon's coat of arms in gilt

on both sides of the binding. He offered this for sixty francs. Like many others, I had telegraphed an order for the book and received the reply that it was already sold. On hearing this story, Mr. Speck grew very excited and expressed the wish that I should try and find out what had happened to the book as he was most anxious to add it to his Goethe collection.

On my return to Europe I endeavored to trace this dealer, but he had left the little town in which he had lived and I could not find out his new address. A few months afterward, in 1927, while staying in Lyons for a day or two I suddenly came across a bookseller's window bearing the name of the bookseller in question. I walked in, introduced myself, and asked him point-blank what had happened to his copy of Napoleon's *Werther*.

He told me that he had sold it just before the catalogue came out, so no one who had ordered it from the catalogue itself had had any chance at all, and that he had even allowed the customer who bought it a special discount of 10 per cent. On being told that I would give him fifty pounds sterling if he would merely give me the name of the collector and if I could get possession of the book, he agreed to give me the man's name and address.

The buyer was the son of a very wealthy and famous Parisian doctor, a member of the French Academy of Medicine. I hesitated to approach the bibliophile directly and employed a solicitor, who was able, after some wearying negotiations, to persuade the possessor to part with it for several hundred pounds.

In the meantime, however, Mr. Speck had died and although Yale University Library was given the opportunity of buying the book to add as a memorial to Mr. Speck and his Goethe collection, the time was unfavorable, and Napoleon's *Werther,* which bore every sign of having been frequently read by him, was sold to the late Mr. Dannie Heineman, the American mathematician and former head of the Sofina Trust in Belgium. The book, with his other treasures, is now in the Yale University Library.

During the same journey in America I was able to sell some very fine illuminated miniatures and books to several art museums,* and I had the pleasant experience of meeting a number of the best-known collectors and library directors. One of these was Mr. William Smith Mason, owner of the greatest collection of Benjamin Franklin books and manuscripts, which he gave to Yale University in 1936. Mr. Mason, who was born in 1867 and died in 1961 at the age of ninety-four, in Rancho Santa Fé, California, also gave a collection of early California history to Pomona College and a Marcus Aurelius collection to the Clements Library, and was active in many historical, literary and bibliophile societies.

On board ship I met again Dr. Harvey Cushing

* Including the famous Toledo, Ohio, Museum of Art, which was then under the direction of that extraordinary genius, Mr. George Stevens.

(1869–1939) the famous brain surgeon, professor of neurology, biographer of William Osler, and collector of a famous medical library; and later, in the States, I met Dr. John Fulton, the head of Yale Historical Medical Library.

I had the pleasure also of meeting in New York that most charming of Yorkshiremen, Arthur Swann, born in Leeds in 1875 and manager, at the age of twenty-five, of William Jaggard's bookshop in Liverpool. In 1902 Arthur Swann was persuaded by John Anderson, Jr., of the American auction firm bearing his name, to join him in New York, where he remained until 1913 as cataloguer of some of the most important book sales that took place in the United States. His most important catalogue was that of the famous Robert Hoe sale in 1911–12. Later, Arthur Swann joined the Parke-Bernet Galleries in New York where he became a director. He died in 1959. He was an adviser in the forming of some of the most famous private libraries in America.

During one of my trips to America I got to know one of the most intelligent and ardent booklovers in the United States, Alfred Ernest Hamill, a man of impeccable taste, born in the same year as myself. Rewarded with a charming wife, he had built a delightful residence at Lake Forest named "Centaurs," which was as beautiful in its conception as in its furnishing. I shall never forget the impression made upon me when I stayed with him and his wife at his Lake Forest home. His library of some ten thousand volumes of the finest specimens of English

literature of the sixteenth, seventeenth and eighteenth centuries was equaled only by another room
filled with the classics and Renaissance literature.
Still another room held the best French literature
and magnificent books on art, architecture, gardening
and costume. His death in 1953 was a great loss to all
who knew him and above all to the Newberry
Library, of Chicago, of which he had been president
for twenty-three years. He was the most truly
civilized man I have ever met.

Another distinguished collector, born in 1862,
was Henry Raup Wagner, who retired from business in 1920 and devoted the rest of his life to
bibliography and history. In 1955, when he was a
mere ninety-three years of age, a bibliography of his
writings listed 167 of his publications, of which all
but six were dated after 1918. Mr. Wagner's special
interest was in American bibliography, although
he began by collecting ten thousand books on
British and Irish economics (now as a gift in the
Yale University Library). He was extremely successful in acquiring books on Mexico, Central and South
America and Spain. This collection of some twenty
thousand items, including over twelve thousand
items on Mexico, went to Yale in 1915. Later he
devoted himself to books on Texas and California,
described by him in his *The Plains and the Rockies*
and *The Spanish Southwest*. These collections also
went to Yale. Mr. Wagner died in 1957. He was the
most charming and knowledgeable of men, and I was
delighted to have made his acquaintance.

Another great collector and great librarian was the late J. Christian Bay, who was born in 1871 in Denmark. After hearing lectures at the University of Copenhagen by the Director of the Missouri Botanical Garden, in St. Louis, he came to St. Louis in 1892 and became an assistant in the Botanical Library. In 1900 he went to the Library of Congress, in Washington. From 1905 to 1947 he was connected with the famous John Crerar Library, in Chicago, becoming its chief librarian in 1928. He had been collecting books on the Midwest, and in 1942 he gave his collection to the State Historical Society of Missouri, at Columbia. He chose Missouri as the final showplace of his Midwestern book collection because of the hospitality he had received in his youth from Dr. William Trelease, the Director of the Botanical Garden, and because he had also met his wife in St. Louis. What Mr. Bay did not know about Americana was not worth knowing.

It is hardly necessary for me to write much about Dr. Abraham Simon Wolf Rosenbach (1876–1952), as so much about him has now been published by Edwin Wolf II and John Fleming, in book form and in an article by the latter in the *Antiquarian Bookman,* October 10, 1953.

It was most pleasant visiting the Rowfant Club, one of the oldest book clubs in America, established on February 29, 1892, by a group of Cleveland book collectors and booklovers who took the name from Rowfant, the home at Crawley, Sussex, of Frederick Locker-Lampson, the leading association book col-

lector of his day. Originally there were sixty resident
and fifteen nonresident members; later the limit was
raised to 150 resident and 55 nonresident members,
and I was fortunate enough, together with King
Manuel, to become a nonresident member. The club
chose the groundhog as its patron saint; and February 2 (Groundhog Day, or Candlemas) was chosen as
the day of the club's annual meeting. In January
1894 the council ordered each member to provide
himself with a candlestick for his exclusive use and
to bear his name, but all candlesticks were to be the
property of the club. When a member dies an ex-
tinguisher is put over the candle as when last used,
and the candlestick is then placed permanently in its
order above the bookcases in the library.

In 1959 the club published *The Rowfant Candlesticks*, by John Calder Pearson, Rowfant librarian
and curator, a quarto volume, limited to 275 copies,
containing 360 photographs of members' candlesticks. In his introductory chapters, Pearson traces
the history of this distinctive Rowfant tradition. A
stuffed-groundhog candleholder is ceremoniously
carried once a year on February 2 by the newly
elected president as a symbol of his office and authority. Each member takes light for his own candle
from that of the president. The Rowfant Club has
no official connection with any outside club. It was
a personal pleasure that in May 1955 seventy-two
club members, wives and daughters, during the club's
pilgrimage to England of two weeks, were able to
visit Oxford and the Bodleian Library.

Mr. Archer Milton Huntington (1870–1955) for many years was the chief buyer of Americana and Spanish books, and my first connection with him was before the First World War. A young Spanish student of architecture, named Salvador Babra, appeared one day in Munich at Ludwig Rosenthal's, bringing with him a large number of books in Spanish and Latin printed in Spain before 1501, and he sold them for what was then a huge price. As these books were extremely rare in Western Europe, a special catalogue was at once printed and sent out to a few collectors, among them Archer Milton Huntington, whose name and address I found among the many thousands of names and addresses in the firm's old index cards. No one seemed to take much notice of the catalogue at first, but one night Ludwig Rosenthal, who was already advanced in years, was called to the telephone from his bed and informed that there was a cable for him from New York; it read: "What discount whole catalogue?" The sender was "Archer Milton Huntington." There was a great temptation to sell the catalogue en bloc, as the total selling price amounted to several thousand pounds, and "Ten per cent" was the answer. The following night Ludwig Rosenthal was aroused from his sleep by another cable, which read: "Discount not sufficient." Cables flew to and fro, till Mr. Huntington sent a final cable ordering the books, and he paid for them immediately!

This was such a pleasant, quick and profitable piece of business that Ludwig Rosenthal, accompanied by one of his sons, left Munich as quickly as possible for Barcelona to rejoin the young Spaniard, who sold him another lot of books. A visit to Madrid brought more books, and another catalogue of Spanish incunabula was sent to Mr. Huntington after a few months. This again was purchased by him en bloc, together with many other fine Spanish works printed after 1501.

At a later date I found out that Mr. Huntington had bought the whole of the famous library of the Marqués de Jérez, of Seville, the brother of the Duc de Tscerclaes. At that time the story was told in Spain that he had paid one million pesetas for the collection and that when King Alfonso XIII rebuked him for buying such important Spanish libraries, Mr. Huntington stopped buying. Today the library and museum of the Hispanic Society of America bear witness to Mr. Archer M. Huntington's wisdom and acumen in his purchases of books and manuscripts and *objets d'art.**

Mr. Huntington reprinted a number of his rare books in facsimile so that the world should also benefit by his treasures, and the curators and librarians of the Hispanic Society of America have always been most generous in allowing scholars to work in the library and make use of the accumulated treasures. He died in December 1955.

* An adopted son of the great railroad builder Collis Potter Huntington, he founded in 1904 the Hispanic Society of America to which he gave a home, an endowment and collections of books and art.

Mr. Archer Milton Huntington's mother, whom I met in her old age when she could hardly see any more, was also a collector of illuminated miniatures. I have already spoken of Mr. Henry Edward Huntington's wonderful collections of books and paintings at San Marino, California.

Chapter XII

A very curious episode, which exercised great influence on the course of book collecting, took place very shortly after the end of the First World War. Just before the war, a Dr. Otto H. F. Vollbehr, of Berlin, a chemist by profession, had made a collection of early books in various languages on the history of the Turks. At the instigation of the Emperor William II, this was purchased from him and presented to the Sultan of Turkey, who shortly afterward entered the war on the side of Germany. Dr. Vollbehr (a fact known to very few) became the astute Chief of the German Secret Service and War Intelligence in the Balkans. His brother, a painter of battle scenes, was a favorite of the Kaiser. His father-in-law was Berlin's Director of Parks and Gardens.

When the First World War ended with the collapse of Germany, Dr. Vollbehr, with his sharp wits, looked round for a means of preserving the family fortune. He took the opportunity of buying up rapidly all the rare American books that were available in the hands of German antiquarian booksellers and put them in the hands of a Leipzig bookseller to sell for foreign currency only—pounds sterling or dollars. A leaflet containing a description of these books came into my hands and, very much against my will, the firm with which I was then connected warmly welcomed Dr. Vollbehr, who had come to London to sell some of his rarities.

So successful was Dr. Vollbehr with this transaction that he resolved to carry on his speculation in books on a very much larger scale, and bethought himself of the opportunity of using his secret connections with the official authorities in Germany to help him in the matter. Having disposed of his Americana, he started buying up all the available books in any language, on any subject, printed before 1501— that is, incunabula, or "cradle books." He scoured the Continent for them and came to England to buy some more. There were plenty of these books on the market at the time, and when he had amassed an enormous quantity of these he traveled to California, where he made use of his German connections to get acquainted with the very rich families of the brewers of German-type beer. Through the local German consul general he made the acquaintance of one of the richest and most important Los Angeles bankers, whom he impressed with his knowledge of early books; and he succeeded in being introduced to Mr. Henry Edward Huntington, who was then making enormous purchases of rare English and early printed books through the Rosenbach Company, of Philadelphia, and George D. Smith, of New York, his favorite agent.

With millions of dollars at his disposal, Mr. Huntington was able to buy Dr. Vollbehr's collection of incunabula, as a fellow collector, giving a very large margin of profit to Vollbehr. So impressed was Dr. Vollbehr by the opportunity now afforded him that he rushed back to Europe and started buying all the finest incunabula, paying very good prices. He bought the first printed book in Portuguese, the *Vita Christi,* in four magnificent volumes, and many other treasures from me.

Back in the United States with the second magnificent collection of choice early printed books, the arrival of which rather startled Mr. Huntington's librarian in chief, he again succeeded in selling these books with a large profit. Not content with two sales of this magnitude, Dr. Vollbehr started buying a third lot of incunabula in Europe, again with the idea of selling these to Mr. Huntington. This time, however, he was too late—Mr. Huntington had died in 1927, and Dr. Vollbehr was faced with the burden of 4,500 volumes including the St. Paul, Carinthia, copy of the Gutenberg Bible on vellum, which were only partly paid for but on which he had secured definite options. At one time Dr. Vollbehr was in despair; he was staying in the same hotel as myself in New York and was unable to meet the Ambassador's bills. In order to help him I bought from him a magnificent copy of the first edition of the Greek *Anthology,* printed on vellum, which I sold on his behalf to Miss Belle da Costa Greene of the Morgan Library, where it was warmly welcomed.

In order to live and carry on his campaign of publicity, Dr. Vollbehr had to mortgage a great portion of his incunabula. He was rescued from a very difficult position, at a time when he was being hard-pressed by booksellers all over Europe for payment, by Representative Ross A. Collins of Mississippi, who in the second session of the 71st Congress, in 1930, introduced a bill for the purchase of the Vollbehr Collection of incunabula for 1½ million dollars. Mr. Collins gave, in 1963, a collection of six scrapbooks containing material relating to the acquisition of its Vollbehr Collection to the Congressional Library.

The incunabula now in the Library of Congress are wanting in the world market, and there are today but few collectors of these first printings, as everyone knows that it is almost impossible, however great the means available for disposal, to form a large collection of such books. Dr. Vollbehr's efforts to make the American public incunabula-minded were managed with great skill!

On one occasion he visited Kansas City and arranged to be interviewed by a representative of the leading local newspaper. The representative was a very charming platinum-blonde (and Dr. Vollbehr was very susceptible to blondes). She, after being told what incunabula were and how Dr. Vollbehr had managed to acquire thousands of such books, asked him unexpectedly, "And what is your favorite book, Dr. Vollbehr?" He naturally replied, with a charming smile, *Gentlemen Prefer Blondes*. I regret to state that the next morning the interview with Dr. Vollbehr was headed: "Dr. Vollbehr's Favorite Incunable, *Gentlemen Prefer Blondes*"!

The subsequent proceedings of Dr. Vollbehr in Germany and the United States do not fall within the scope of my memoirs, but I have been reliably informed that before the Second World War, Dr. Vollbehr's activities in Washington in behalf of the Nazis were regarded by the American government with grave suspicion.

The hearings of the Congressional committee on the purchase of the incunabula collection provided some fun for librarians and antiquarian booksellers. The speech of the Honorable Ross A. Collins made in the House of Representatives on Friday, February 7, 1930, and reprinted on seven quarto pages in double columns from the *Congressional Record* is now a collector's desideratum. The leaflet gives a very full account of the Vollbehr Collection, the Gutenberg Bible and the evaluation of the collection by experts, including the present writer.

When Dr. Herbert Putnam, the eminent Librarian of Congress, urged the committee to purchase the collection, especially because of the possibility of obtaining one of the few remaining available copies of the Gutenberg Bible, one of the members of the committee said, "What? I never knew the Bible was written by Gutenberg. Are you sure of your facts?" This true story does not figure in the leaflet.

On one occasion Dr. Vollbehr, who was staying in London with his wife at the Savoy, invited my two chiefs and myself to have lunch with him at his hotel. Toward the end of the meal, after having imbibed perhaps a little more than usual, and in the excitement at having purchased a large number of very rare and perhaps unique early printed books, Dr. Vollbehr lifted his glass of wine and suddenly shouted: "Ah, *der Tag!* The day will come when we shall smash you, our enemies." My two chiefs did not know to what he was referring and he was immediately hushed up by his wife, who obviously knew that her husband had in mind the long-projected German war of revenge on England. This outburst was indeed a revelation to me of the German state of mind and love of violence.

Among American collectors who were single-minded in the pursuit of their speciality, I would like to name Mr. George Arents, who, as a director of the American Tobacco Company, decided to buy every item called to his attention referring to smoking and the use of tobacco. This collection, which is now one of the many prizes of the New York Public Library, was fully described in a series of folio volumes published for Mr. Arents by the Rosenbach Company. In addition to books which have tobacco as their main concern, Mr. Arents was persuaded to buy every obtainable early English play which mentioned smoking and the use of tobacco in pipes. Thus, the collection comprises a large number of early English plays and pamphlets which no longer come on the market and which, in addition to his own special interest in them, are of great importance for the study of the English language and English customs.

One of the most learned of bibliophiles was the late Fritz Kreisler, prince of violinists, who invariably came to see me to share a lunch when he was in England. He collected books not for the pleasure of being able to boast that he possessed such and such an edition of a great author or the product of a famous press, but because he was stirred to the depths by being able to read in the first edition the Latin and Greek classics in which he was steeped.

He was surely unique among musicians with his classical education. He was all the more to be esteemed when, with a broken heart, he decided to sell his cherished books in New York and to use the money realized by such a sale, for the benefit of the victims of Nazi Germany.

On my first visit to California I was invited by Mrs. George Millard (a famous bookseller agent of California millionaires) to a country club, where I was tempted to indulge in some delightful-looking asparagus. However, appearances were deceptive, and the asparagus, far from being grown in California, must have come from a tainted tin. In consequence I was laid up at the beautiful Vista Del Arroyo Hotel, at Pasadena, with a severe attack of food poisoning, which kept me out of action for a number of days.

Owing to this absence from normal life, I was unable to accept an invitation of Mr. William

Andrews Clark, Jr., son of the famous Senator Clark of Montana, to attend the special exhibition in his home of his treasured first editions and Shakespeare quartos. His library was as famous in its way as the collection made by his elder brother, Charles W. Clark, of incunabula, early French books and other rarities. The invited guests were shown the treasures that were laid out for their inspection by Mr. William Clark's librarian, Mr. Robert Ernest Cowan, author of several bibliographies, by Mr. Clark's niece, who also acted as librarian, and by Mr. Clark himself.

When I met Mr. Clark's niece again after my recovery she told me how much I had missed, and she related the following story:

Mr. William Clark was showing his great collection of Shakespeare quartos to a Senator's wife, who, having only a little knowledge, exclaimed, "How wonderful! Were they all printed by Caxton?"

The beautiful building built for Mr. Clark with its elaborate Dryden mosaics and its contents is now the property of the University of California.

Chapter XIII

In 1931 I paid my first and only visit to Russia, a visit which lasted a fortnight. The reason for the journey was that the world market for antiques, rare coins and valuable books was being increasingly disturbed by the sudden and seemingly entirely unregulated influx of incunabula, French eighteenth-century books and bindings which the Soviet authorities were pouring into Austria and Germany for sale. In the same way they had deluged the market with platinum in 1919 and thus forced down the price of that precious metal, of which Russia had formerly enjoyed a monopoly.

During the years 1930–1932 the Russian government had come into possession, through the nationalization of imperial and private collections, of great quantities of unwanted or duplicate artistic and literary treasures for which they had no special use.

This haphazard disposal of wonderful paintings, furniture, coins and books which were being sent to the auction rooms in France, Germany and England, was not in the interest either of the U.S.S.R. or of the collectors and dealers. When suddenly three or four copies of the first edition of Homer and several duplicate copies of the very rarest French eighteenth-century books were being offered for sale at one fell swoop, it was felt advisable to prevent the flooding of the market, which was bringing down prices and which was to the advantage of no one. A suggestion was made by me to the firm with which I was then connected and to Messrs. Sotheby, the London auctioneers, that it would be of mutual interest to give some sound advice personally by going to the department in Leningrad or Moscow which was responsible for the disposal of surplus artistic and literary treasures.

In 1931 a deputation of three, of which I formed part, offered to go to Moscow with a view to reorganizing the movement of such goods and arranging the proper distribution of such treasures so that they would be sent to the countries in which they would be most salable. It seemed ridiculous, for instance, that nineteenth-century German coins were being sent to the London auction rooms, while French eighteenth-century bindings and literary works were sent to Vienna.

Our offer to help was accepted by the Russian authorities, and the three of us, of whom I am the only living member, left for Moscow via Poland. We traveled independently of Intourist, the Russian travel bureau, and agreed to meet in Berlin, where one of my companions, being late, just managed to jump onto the through train to Poland as it was already leaving the station.

Before leaving London I had taken some twenty

lessons in Russian conversation and wrote out what I thought would be the most useful phrases, such as: "Please give me a cup of tea." "Have you any plain-boiled potatoes?" "May I have some plain-boiled fish?" "Have you any illuminated manuscripts?" Unfortunately, those lessons proved of little avail when we got to Russia, as we found that the country was suffering from hunger. There were no potatoes, there was no tea, and there was very little fish.

On our way into Russia, we had to change trains at the Polish-Soviet frontier, and we had no difficulty whatsoever with the customs. We were surprised to find a dining car decorated with elaborate wood carvings and beautifully appointed with original oil paintings; later on we found out that it was part of a private train which had belonged to a pre-Revolutionary Russian millionaire. One of my companions was very thirsty and on seeing a decanter on the table he poured out a tumblerful of what he took to be water; but, unfortunately for him, it turned out to be vodka—absolutely colorless but not painless!

On our arrival at Moscow we had great difficulty in getting from the station to the hotel where rooms had been booked for us. Very kindly an employee of Intourist who happened to be making an inquiry at the railway station saw our plight and offered to take us in his omnibus. At that time in the whole of Moscow there were only about four taxis, very different from what I believe is the case today.

At that time, too, almost everything was rationed;

nothing could be bought by the ordinary man in the street without a card and proof that he had not already in his possession an item such as he now wanted to buy; boots and clothes were very scarce. The only unrationed goods we saw on sale in the shops in Moscow, and later on in Leningrad during our stay there, were coats of armor and outsize French nineteenth-century marble clocks.

All food was rationed, and the chief aim of all Russians was to get something to eat. We were once welcomed at one of the Russian government departments with a little ersatz tea and some small cakes which we could not swallow; they seemed to be made of sand, not of flour. In the museums, the attendants, chiefly aged women, seemed to be privileged; they could be seen attending to their duties, watching visitors and munching plain black bread, deeming themselves lucky to have something with which to fill their stomachs. There were no restaurants of any kind, and I was exceedingly fortunate in having brought enough tins of sardines with me to last the fortnight we stayed in Russia.

There were, however, plenty of new bookshops, and these were crowded with would-be customers, as there was not much else on which the inhabitants could spend their money. All the bookshops were for new books only, and they sold just one class of book. There were no old books for sale.

The country through which we had traveled, in Germany, Poland and Russia, was covered with snow to a great depth, but we arrived in Moscow just as the ice was breaking up on the Moskva River, late in April. This breaking-up of the ice was heralded as the beginning of spring.

On the first night in Moscow I was already in my pajamas and about to go to bed, when the telephone rang and a feminine voice asked in French if I was there. As I knew nobody in Moscow I was very much surprised and asked, "Who are you?" The reply, in quite passable French, explained that the lady (presumably young) felt very lonely as her friend had left her for France and she wondered whether I would like to have her company. I was very annoyed and used one of my few Russian phrases, "Go to the devil."

The next day I complained to the hotel manager, who had come to visit me to inquire whether he could be of any service to me—and to beg me to let him have a few stiff collars and some ties. He explained that hotel management was not really his business and that he had formerly been manager of the Leningrad Opera; he had been chosen to manage the chief hotel for foreign visitors in Moscow because he knew several languages.

I told the manager that it was only through the connivance of the hotel porter that anybody could have known of my arrival. He was unable to counter this. On comparing notes at a later date with other visitors to Russia, I found that this matter of the night telephone call was a regular part of the secret-police method of keeping a check on foreign visitors through their female accomplices.

After a few days in Moscow we experienced difficulty in meeting the responsible head or commissar of the Department of Foreign Trade whom we wished to interview and advise. In order to use our time in Russia to the best purpose, we took the train to Leningrad, where we visited the museum and picture gallery of the Hermitage. We admired especially the remarkable collections of paintings and *objets d'art* which had been bought for Catherine the Great in London and Paris in the eighteenth century. The treasures in the museums were astounding.

As we found ourselves in Leningrad with time to spare before our return to Moscow, we visited the government department for the export of books and antiques. We found that the man in charge of the books, though not the director of the whole department, was a former Austrian subject, who, before he left his native Hungary, was a well-known collector of porcelain. We were shown a number of large folio natural-history books of flowers, birds, et cetera, but as they were imperfect we did not care to buy any of them. They were not then as easy to dispose of or as valuable as they would be today, when single color plates of the kind are extensively used for decoration of apartments.

After this refusal the Hungarian exclaimed, "How was it that you timed your visit to Russia and to Leningrad in such an extraordinary way that you arrived here on the very day that we received from the former Imperial Library in this city a Gutenberg Bible for disposal?" It was the only copy in Russia;

it had been a duplicate possession of the Munich State Library and still bore the disposal marks of that famous institution. A price was named (a reasonable price in those days), and we at once sold it by cable to the famous Swiss collector Dr. Martin Bodmer, whose private collection of world literature is unique.

On another day, thinking that there would be an exhibition of rare and fine books in showcases, as in the British Museum, we paid a visit to the nationalized Imperial Public Library, from which the Gutenberg Bible had come. We met Mr. Bloch, the keeper of manuscripts, who was then celebrating his jubilee as keeper. There was no special exhibition of rare printed books, but in the manuscript department there were a few glass cases containing almost entirely manuscripts, and in addition to items of Russian interest there was on view the last Prayer Book of Mary Queen of Scots, with fine illuminated miniatures. I then noticed that in a dark corner of the room there was a lectern on which stood a large square leather box, with a leather cover over it lettered "Codex Sinaiticus Petropolitanus." When the cover was lifted one page of this famous manuscript was visible, but that was all. I called the attention of my two companions (who had never heard of the Codex before) to this treasure and pointed out the extraordinary interest attached to this, the earliest complete, or practically complete, manuscript of the Old and New Testaments, written on vellum, in large uncial Greek letters in the first half of the fourth century.

This manuscript had a long history, which I will try to render in a few sentences only. In May 1844, a German Biblical scholar named Konstantin von Tischendorf (1815–1874), visiting the famous Monastery of St. Catherine, on Mount Sinai, for the first time, noticed in the hall a large basket filled with old leaves of vellum containing some very early Greek writing which the librarian informed him were to be burned as rubbish. Among this heap of fragments, Tischendorf found some 129 leaves of the Old Testament in Greek, which seemed to him the oldest he had ever seen. The monks allowed him to take away one third of the leaves; he later presented these to the University Library at Leipzig.

He was able to revisit the monastery in 1853, but the monks could not, or would not, tell him anything of the manuscript. On a third visit, in the year 1859, the steward of the monastery took down from a shelf over his cell door (which was chiefly used for the storage of spare coffee cups) a bulky parcel, which he untied, revealing not merely the rest of the leaves which Tischendorf had rescued from the wastepaper basket some fifteen years before, but other parts of the Old Testament and the complete New Testament. Being unable, before his departure, to copy more than the Epistle of Barnabas. Tischendorf was, however, able to persuade the monks to send the manuscript to a branch Greek monastery in Cairo, where, in the space of two months, he copied it completely. Soon, it became very obvious to him that a mere copy of a manuscript of this early date was quite insufficient for scholarly purposes and he suggested to the monks on Mount Sinai that they should present the original manuscript to the head of the Orthodox Church of Russia, namely, the Russian Tsar.

After some difficulties this project took shape. In consideration of a promotion in the Church for the head of the monastery, plus a number of Russian decorations and the sum of nine thousand rubles in cash (£1,350), Tischendorf was allowed to take the manuscript himself to Russia and place it, on November 19, 1859, in the hands of Tsar Alexander II. The Codex was at first deposited in the Foreign Office at St. Petersburg, and it was many years before it was transferred to the Imperial Public Library in the same city, where it was stored on the lectern in the manuscript department. Photographic facsimiles were published of both Testaments by the Oxford University Press just before the First World War.

On our return to Moscow we tried to conclude our negotiations with the Russian Department for Foreign Trade and to give them the benefit of our advice as to the disposal of their superfluous literary and artistic treasures. We were then at last able to meet the Vice-Commissar for Foreign Trade, who became very interested in our suggestions and explained to me that he had become a civil servant in the Foreign Trade Department because he had been a very successful Quartermaster General of the Red Army in Turkestan, with headquarters at Bokhara. He asked me what we had seen in Leningrad, and I told him of the Italian paintings, the Greek colored Tanagra statuettes and the Scythian silver which we had admired at the Hermitage. As a joke, I told him that we had also visited the Ex-Imperial Library and had seen there a manuscript which, if he ever needed money, he could arrange to tie up in a piece of strong brown paper and send with an invoice to me in London. He asked what this manuscript was and I told him the Codex Sinaiticus Petropolitanus. He had, of course, never heard of this famous early Greek manuscript Bible, and I took the opportunity of explaining to him very briefly what it was.

The story of the Codex would have ended here, if two years later, in the autumn of 1933, the Hungarian, on a mission from Leningrad, and again offering first editions of Homer in London, had not asked me one day point-blank whether I thought the Codex Sinaiticus was worth a million pounds. I replied that the Codex might well be worth a million pounds or a million dollars, but that I knew of no one who had this sum at his disposal and would be willing to spend it for such a purpose. The inquiry, however, led me to ask if indeed the Codex was now for sale, and I assured him that if his chiefs ever wanted to sell it at a reasonable price I would be glad to find a buyer for him.

A few weeks later the Russian cultural attaché in Paris, Comrade Ilyin, informed me that the Russian government was prepared to sell the manuscript, through him, for two hundred thousand pounds, and that we could claim a commission if we were successful in finding a buyer. At that time the press was full of accounts of the new Liverpool Roman Catholic Cathedral which was being built and was to cost one million pounds. I inquired from my old friend the famous typographer Stanley Morison if he could tell me who was paying for the building. I gave him the reason for my inquiry, namely, that I thought the Codex exhibited in the newest cathedral would prove a great attraction and by its very age would make up for the modernity of the building. I told Morison that I had an option on the Codex Sinaiticus and he asked me whether he might mention that fact to Sir Frederic Kenyon, the then retired director of the British Museum, and president of the Friends of the National Libraries.

Within twenty-four hours Sir Frederic Kenyon came to see me and inquire whether this option of two hundred thousand pounds on the manuscript was a fact. He went away reassured, saying that he would see some friends and find out what could be done.

The following day, he came back with instructions to me to make a definite offer on his behalf for the manuscript, but the offer was, unfortunately, only forty thousand pounds, a fifth of the sum that had been asked. I protested against this inappropriate offer, but he urged me to transmit the offer. I wrote to Paris and received, as expected, a scathing reply. On being informed of this, Sir Frederic again asked for an opportunity to consult his friends and returned with an offer of fifty thousand pounds—which was again refused.

However, in his reply Mr. Ilyin said that he would like to show that he was in earnest about the sale and reduced the price by ten per cent, to the sum of one hundred and eighty pounds. Sir Frederic, after a further consultation with his friends, returned with an offer of sixty thousand pounds, which was again refused. I was afraid that this haggling would annoy Mr. Ilyin so much that he would break off the negotiations altogether and then sell the manuscript elsewhere. I therefore urged Sir Frederic to make the very best offer, on a take-it-or-leave-it basis. I was pleasantly surprised when he came back with a final offer of one hundred thousand pounds.

I passed the offer on, and in the next communication from Paris Mr. Ilyin explained that he was a married man and that his wife was most anxious to visit England—"the land of her dreams"—and that both he and Mrs. Ilyin, having applied to the British Passport Office in Paris, had been refused visas. He intimated that if he and his wife could come to England on a visit it might be easier to negotiate the sale of the Codex.

I thereupon rang up my old friend John (now Sir John) Balfour, who had been a prisoner with me in Ruhleben Civilian Internment Camp and was then working at the Foreign Office between two posts abroad, and I informed him of the situation. He immediately telephoned to Paris, visas were secured for Mr. and Mrs. Ilyin, and I had the pleasure of letting Sir Frederic Kenyon face Mr. Ilyin, thus bringing the matter to a successful conclusion.

Now Mr. Ilyin had to secure his own position and to obtain the consent of the Department for Foreign Trade in Moscow. This was not an easy matter, as there was then no direct telephone between London and Moscow and the conversation had to be relayed via Paris. Another difficulty was the fact that no one in Moscow was willing to risk his neck by taking responsibility for this important sale.

However, after a few days the consent of the Russian Government was definitely given, and Prime Minister Mr. Ramsay MacDonald, who was one of the two friends referred to by Sir Frederic Kenyon (the other was the Archbishop of Canterbury), made a statement in Parliament that the government was arranging to buy the Codex Sinaiticus under the condition that the public should make a contribution to the cost price. As a matter of fact, the public subscribed over sixty thousand pounds, so the government really had a bargain in the fourth-century Codex Sinaiticus, now bearing the press mark "British Museum Additional MS. 43725."

It was not long before the London evening papers were able to print posters which read "CODEX ARRIVES IN LONDON"; and the "twopenny Tube" as we used to call the Central London Railway, printed large posters reproducing a page of the manuscript, with the indication that the Tottenham Court Road and the British Museum Stations were the appropriate stations to be used when one went to see the Codex.

The Codex reached its home in the British Museum on December 27, 1933. I arranged for newsreel cameramen and newspaper photographers to take pictures of its arrival at the offices of the Russian Trade Delegation at Bush House, Strand. The Soviet officials were amazed at the sudden invasion of their premises by dozens of newsmen.

Since many threatening letters had been received by the British Museum authorities from persons who protested the spending of so much money with the Russians at a time when there were more than one million unemployed in this country, I arranged for two detectives from Vine Street Police Station to accompany the delivery of the manuscript. As the *Daily Express* had given a considerable amount of publicity to the purchase and arrival of the Codex, I arranged for one of their reporters, Miss Margaret Lane, not then as famous as she is today, to accompany us and the manuscript to the British Museum.

On reaching Great Russell Street we found the great steps leading to the entrance crowded with people awaiting the arrival of the Codex. As one rather villainous-looking detective emerged from our car carrying the shapeless bundle of the Codex wrapped in brown paper in his arms, every male in the crowd bared his head! As we proceeded to the office of the director, Sir George Hill, to hand over the manuscript, there was a great rush in the Museum corridors, and one of the two detectives asked, "Is it safe to leave the manuscript here?"

To my amazement the British Museum authorities too had arranged to have the arrival of the manuscript photographed for the newsreels—the first time that such an event was allowed in the Museum. Unfortunately, however, the picturemaking was a failure.

Among the letters which reached the Museum complaining about the purchase, one came from a workman in the photographic trade who wrote that he could not understand when such good cameras were being manufactured daily in England, that it was necessary to spend one hundred thousand pounds on a Russian "Kodak"! Another letter was from two old ladies in the country who warned the keeper of manuscripts to be very, very careful when he had the Codex translated because they suspected that the Russian government had crossed out all the "nots" in the Ten Commandments!

On the whole, the press was very favorable to the purchase, and so popular were the visits to the British Museum to see the Codex that there were long queues of people waiting their turn and clutching coins, bank notes and checks to put into the money-box to help with the purchase. The Russians handed the manuscript to us in London without any previous payment, and within a fortnight the Treasury issued an order for payment of the full amount, without waiting for the public's contributions. Within twelve months we were provided with over five thousand clippings from newspapers all over the world by Dunant's Press Cutting Agency, and there was no country in which the transfer of the Codex to a permanent home in England was not welcomed.

Chapter XIV

Toward the end of May 1940, when there was very little official news in Paris about the German invasion of France, I met by chance M. Maurice Devries, an advertising specialist whose acquaintance I had made through the ingenious way in which he exercised his profession. He specialized in providing publicity presents to be sent on New Year's Day to all the better-known French physicians from the manufacturers of patent medicines. For some years he had produced annually admirably reproduced selections of facsimiles of historical autographs, which he chose wherever opportunity offered, either in private collections or in public libraries. One of his friends was the famous general of the Salonica expedition in the First World War, Marshal Franchet d'Esperey.

I asked him how he was, and he told me that he had just met his friend the Marshal, who had told him that all was not well and that the German armies were very much nearer Paris than was reported in the French press or on the wireless. I thought the matter over and decided to make a selection of the most valuable books in stock and remove the business temporarily as far from Paris as possible, preferably to Biarritz, where there was already a reasonable number of possible customers, including the pick of French society. I ordered a checkup for my outsize Lincoln car, which I had not used during the winter, and suggested to my younger son and our expert lady bibliographer that they should move with me to Biarritz. Both refused, and I left as soon as possible, on May 30, 1940.

After arriving at Biarritz on May 31 and finding a room at a hotel, I set about looking for a printer who could be trusted to make a fine job of a catalogue of the important books which I had brought with me. I deposited the money I had brought with me from Paris into a local branch of Barclay's Bank and while searching for a printer in Biarritz and Bayonne, which was the nearest big town, the news became worse. Then the Fall of Paris was announced.

I looked to escape from France and applied to a colleague and special friend of mine in Madrid to help me. There was no British consul in Biarritz and no Portuguese or Spanish consul. My first thought, of course, was to go to Lisbon via Spain and return to England. I sent my son a wire to Paris asking him to join me and awaited events.

A week after we had heard that the Germans had entered Paris my son arrived, having made the journey from Paris in about eight days partly on a bicycle, partly on foot, partly by train, partly kneeling on the spare wheel on the back of a two-seater car, originally evacuated from Brussels and driven from Tours by the British consul in Paris, and partly on a postman's omnibus. My son's luggage consisted of a small attaché case in which he had placed some of the firm's ledgers and a very valuable eighteenth-century French binding which had been ordered by an Argentine client.

Immediately he arrived we went to Bayonne to visit the British consul. He turned out to be a Dane, who advised us that within a few days there would be a 50-ton fishing boat to take British subjects back to England. This risky voyage over the Bay of Biscay in a tiny boat did not appeal to me, and I still had no answer from Spain.

Calling on the Spanish and Portuguese consuls I found that they were playing Box and Cox—each of them professed that he would be delighted to give us a visa to enter his country provided that his colleague would give us his visa first!

By accident I had to call on Barclay's Bank to fetch some money and overheard two of the British cashiers talking about what they were going to do the following evening. They planned to leave Biarritz on June 17 for Bordeaux to return to England. I questioned them and they told me that a ship would be waiting for British subjects at Bordeaux on the following day. The question was how to get to Bordeaux before the Germans got there. Fortunately, the car in which I had come to Biarritz was garaged in the neighborhood, but the difficulty was to get a chauffeur to take us to Bordeaux, as neither my son nor I was able to drive the car. The chauffeur whom I had hired to bring me to Biarritz was fully employed there by a member of French society and could not leave his employers during the day. However, I persuaded him to drive through the night to Bordeaux and, if necessary, return before dawn to Biarritz.

We left in the late afternoon of June 17 and passed the gendarmerie station on the outskirts of Bordeaux, taking with us the regrets and apologies of the officer in charge, who expressed his shame at our having to leave France because France could no longer protect us from the German invaders. We expected to be stopped by the military on the way to Bordeaux, by either French or German soldiers, but, to our surprise, we entered Bordeaux without a single challenge and found the streets empty. We drove straight to the waterfront and looked for the ship which we imagined would be waiting there as mentioned by the Barclay's Bank cashiers. There was, however, no ship visible, and we therefore made at once for a hotel in which I had been a guest some years before. There we were graciously allowed to spend the night in armchairs in the vestibule, as the hotel was completely filled up. I must not forget to state that the French government had by that time left Tours and moved to Bordeaux.

Although it was already after midnight, my son, with the car and chauffeur, decided to go to the British consulate; there he found the officials and some naval officers packing, and he was told by them that there would indeed be a boat next day to take us all to England. We were told to bring our own food, as the boat would probably not have enough for all who would be on board. Not long after his return to the hotel the Germans started bombing Bordeaux to induce Marshal Pétain and his government to confirm the shameful armistice that was pending.

The hotel guests, including ourselves, descended into the wine cellars and after some delay returned to where we were before. Next morning we called at the British consulate and were given slips of paper authorizing us to a cross-Channel passage on a certain British ship. We at once started to look for provisions and found a grocer's shop, where we were able to buy some tins of sardines, chocolate, bananas and a box or two of cheese, the well-known "Vache qui rit."

We were told to take a very early train from Bordeaux which would bring us to Le Verdon, at the mouth of the Gironde River. We were amazed to see that along the whole length of the waterfront there were abandoned cars, including many Daimlers and Rolls-Royces, completely empty; but there was no ship there. We were urged, however, to get out of the train to board a curious kind of steam lighter, which apparently had been awaiting us for a long time. On this narrow platform the whole trainload of passengers crowded together—men, women and children; not only British, but apparently a number of other European nationalities; men from the Y.M.C.A., et cetera, et cetera.

The captain of the lighter with his full load then left the quayside and started circling the harbor looking for a boat on which to discharge us, but in vain.

Some on board the lighter thought the captain was either drunk or a traitor, to judge from the way he was wasting much precious time looking for a non-existent ship. However, after a fruitless search which lasted nearly an hour, he ascertained that the boat for which he was looking had already left the night before, thus leaving him with a cargo of un-happy, homeless passengers. In view of this unfortu-nate occurrence he decided to try to get rid of us in driblets and approached the S.S. *Madura* (an old P. and O. liner) whose Captain agreed to take one hundred of his burden as passengers. As we drew nearer to the *Madura,* to unload the first hundred, three German planes appeared and started to drop their unwelcome bombs. One of the planes was shot down by a British destroyer that happened to be near, and the other two planes then flew away.

We scrambled on board and found a sailor who allotted us a place in a passageway where we could lie down on the deck; there were no longer any berths available. The ship had entered the French waters with ninety-five passengers; shortly after we got on board it left with about 1,900. The S.S. *Madura* was dangerously overloaded, meals were taken in seven sittings, decks and passageways were littered with passengers, and there were lifeboats for only about four hundred. The passengers included a large number of Poles and Frenchmen, who were shortly to become the nucleus of the Free Polish and Free French Forces. The crew of Lascars were most unselfish and sacrificed their rations of tea and rice for the passengers. As we had brought our own food, we renounced any claim to be fed.

Among the passengers on board were Baron and Baroness de Rothschild from their vineyards of Château-Lafite, near Bordeaux, several members of the British consulate staff in Paris and their families, and the English and American war correspondents, most of whom slept on deck.

After an uneventful passage, which lasted some thirty-six hours, we had the pleasure of arriving at Falmouth on the twentieth of June, safe and unhurt although the boat had no protection on the way from France. The sea, even in the Bay of Biscay, was as smooth as a millpond and the weather delightfully sunny. The other ship that sailed in company with the S.S. *Madura* was a prison ship which had also been ordered to put into Le Verdon to take aboard refugees.

After having seen in Paris the arrival of the refugees from Strasbourg, Alsace, Belgium and the French provinces, and at Biarritz having seen the arrival of the refugees from Paris, we ourselves had become refugees in our own country. At Falmouth we found triumphal arches awaiting us and omnibuses to take us to a public amusement park, where we were fed by the W.V.S. on fool provided free of charge and voluntarily by the local bakers, grocers and other donors. We were greatly affected by our welcome and by the kindness of the volunteer ladies, and to my surprise, I was even offered, by one of the officers of the British Custom Service in attendance at the park, his own bed at his home. The amusement park in Falmouth was in fact an official compound, which one could not leave until one had been cleared by the security services. If one had a valid British passport, as we, of course, had, this was fairly straightforward; and next morning we were free to leave after medical inspection and could return to our homes.

I shall always feel grateful to those two cashiers whom I had the good fortune to overhear in Barclay's Bank discussing their plans for returning to England via Bordeaux. After having been a prisoner of the Germans for four years from November 1914 to November 1918, I did not wish to fall into their hands once again to meet with the inevitable fate that they meted out to their unfortunate victims.

Epilogue

The time has now come for me to put an end to the recording of my "ramblings." I am writing this within a month of attaining my eighty-third birthday, and during the years that have passed so many things have happened to me, I have visited so many countries, and met so many people, that I must now call a halt.

If I had followed on the road which had been made easy for me by my family connections I should have entered the banking profession or the trade in precious stones, but, as it happened, I was able to choose my own path, and I have never had any reason to regret having followed it from my early youth, although, instead of becoming a publisher, I became an "antiquarian" bookseller.

In no other profession would it have been possible for me, as a simple commoner, to have been made a friend of a king and to have been on such amicable terms with queens, princes, princesses and dukes, with ambassadors, with millionaires and with men of letters.

I could have written at length of many adventures,

but bearing in mind what I have already hinted at in my preface, I have deliberately decided to omit many of them which might, in some way, have displeased or even offended the individuals with whom I was in professional contact.

During the course of many years in any one profession one is bound to meet some villains, though I must say that on the whole I have not encountered many.

In the profession of bookselling itself there were few villains though naturally, being human, some of them had faults; but, by and large, in whatever country I was, I nearly always found that my colleagues were, even if eccentric, individuals of some standing and sound principles, anxious to help their colleagues and their customers.

I have often been asked how one achieves success as a bookseller. In a specialist monthly newsletter published in Chislehurst, Kent, and entitled *Selling,* in an article by Stuart Thomson, I find the recipe for success: "Success is achieved by unmitigating hard work, constant attention to detail, exercising considerable moral courage in overcoming the disappointments, being cooperative and helpful to his colleagues and being dedicated to his job, because he loves it. It is this affection which provides him with enthusiasm."

When asked by collectors why they should collect, I can only give them this hint from Thoreau, which curiously enough I have found in the same newsletter: "The truly great book teaches one better than to read it. I must soon lay it down and commence living on its hints . . . what I began by reading, I must finish by acting."

Appendix

LETTERS TO THE AUTHOR
FROM KING MANUEL OF PORTUGAL

Schloss Sigmaringen
14. XI. 1927

MY DEAR DR. ETTINGHAUSEN,

Overburdened with work and "overwhelmed" by a mountain of letters and telegrams, not to mention matters which I must study and decide upon, I have been unable to find the necessary peace and quietness to reply to your letters of the 7th, 9th and 10th November. There is so much to consider that I must ask you in advance to excuse the telegraphic style which I shall be using.

[Your] letter of the 7th.

I have taken note of the different newspaper cuttings, the letter in the *Star* etc. You were quite right: but one must be prepared to listen to and to read many other stupid things, not to mention false rumors. I am very happy that you can await my return, because for my part, also, I am very anxious to talk to you and to arrange several important matters. We leave here on the 18th for Munich (Hotel Vier Jahreszeiten). . . .

If you need anything you can telegraph either to the above address or to Munich: on the evening of the 19th we are taking the Orient Express for Paris, where we shall arrive Sunday the 20th at 11 A.M. As usual we shall be staying at the Ritz, probably until Wednesday 23rd, the probable date of our return to Fulwell Park. If I can do anything for you write to me to the Ritz. . . .

As to the books of the Esperança Library and the Chagas Library, we will talk about them when I am back. If, as I hope, I reach Fulwell on the evening of the 23rd I shall telephone you on the morning of the 24th: the saving of a day for you; and I may perhaps go to London to see you that same afternoon. As to the manuscripts, please send them at once to Miss Withers (the originals and the typed copies) so that she can immediately begin to revise them and take special care to mark the accents correctly: I have written a long letter giving full instructions to Miss Withers. I have asked her at the same time to telephone you so as to arrange everything with you. No doubt there are at Fulwell some Portuguese manuscripts which are ready but I am afraid that the majority are "rather late," that is to say, after 1545, the date which I believe will terminate the first volume. But Miss Withers will be able to give you a full explanation: I have told her about what [bibliographies] you are going to send to Fulwell for the Hebrew books, Haebler, etc.

You can very well imagine that as an ardent book-lover I am very anxiously awaiting the news of the *Marco Polo:* I am sure that the manuscript which was brought from Venice by the Infante Dom Pedro for his brother [Henry] the Navigator must have made a profound impression upon him. I can assure you that the idea of possessing this magnificent book makes no less an impression upon me; and now in addition to all this you have written to me that there is a possibility of obtaining the *Glosa Famosissima* printed by V. Fernandes in 1501: Doctor, you are an extraordinary person and "I take my hat off to you"!! I think I have now answered your letter of the 7th.

[*Your*] *letter of November 9th.*

I have read the proposed prospectus in French. As you have asked me, I have taken the liberty of making some slight corrections. One sentence which I have marked is really excellent. It seems to me that the whole "answers the purpose" perfectly.

[*Your*] *letter of November 10th.*

I have read very carefully what you have written to me, my dear friend, you know much better than I do what should be done as regards Brazil. . . . I only found it interesting to let you know what the Conde de Penha Garcia wrote me. There is no doubt that far-reaching results can be obtained by far-reaching propaganda: but you know also that personal influence and propaganda can also sometimes prove important. I am convinced that a person like Colonel Hull can be of great help in Brazil. It would be very useful if we could have several more like him! As soon as I return I shall be very happy to receive Colonel Hull's visit and to show him my library: he may be an excellent "Publicity Agent"! We shall have to talk about this.

I must add that you have done the right thing in asking Miss Withers for the *Castanheda*. I think I have now replied to your letters but I must not forget to tell you how happy I am to hear that the barometer is rising—183 subscriptions, that is already a nice number, and if the barometer continues to rise as quickly as this we shall soon have 200. I have also some interesting news to give you.

My mother has talked to the King of Spain in Naples about my book, and about the promise he gave me in London to arrange for some publicity in Spain. He was profoundly apologetic that he had failed to do so: but said he had not forgotten his promise and that having been away from Madrid nearly all the time, it had been impossible for him, but that as soon as he returned, which would be immediately, he would busy himself with the matter.

I also asked my mother to find out from her sister, the Duchess of Aosta, if something could be done in Italy either in the way of propaganda or by obtaining subscriptions. I am awaiting her answer.

But this is what will interest you most: I have just received from Lisbon a letter from Senhor de Sequeira, my General Administrator. He tells me that he has just had a meeting (arranged by General Rosado, the [Portuguese] Ambassador in London, who has been several weeks in Lisbon) with Dr. Júlio Dantas* about the books which belong

* President of the Portuguese Academy of Sciences and Inspector-General of Portuguese Libraries and Archives.

to me and which are in the Library at Ajuda. Dr. Júlio Dantas was extremely amiable and his amiability went so far as to inform Senhor de Sequeira what phrases he should use in his Request. This having now been done we shall see what will be the result, but in any case it is interesting: we shall talk about it in London because if you come to Lisbon you may be able to see Dr. Júlio Dantas.

I am now concluding this enormous letter. I am very anxious to be at home quietly and to be working. We shall not leave home (unless it is absolutely necessary) for several months and certainly not before the middle of April.

I do not want to stir from home before all my work for the publication of Volume I is completed.

Again thank you for your letters. I beg you, my dear Doctor, to believe me,

Your very devoted
MANUEL R.

P.S. It is extremely cold here, it has been snowing hard for three days in addition to a continuous icy wind.

Fulwell Park, Twickenham
26. XII. 1927

MY DEAR DR. ETTINGHAUSEN,

Thank you for your telegrams and your *very interesting* letter. As usual, you have accomplished much in a very short time: as usual also, I am awaiting your return impatiently. I am very happy that you have seen Senhor Malheiro Dias: we could not have a better "Publicity Agent" in Brazil; he is a remarkably intelligent man and a most valuable writer who exercises great influence. In your letter you tell me also that you have seen the Conde de Penha Garcia, Senhor D'Ornellas* and Senhor de Sequeira. I am very pleased to hear of this: have you also seen D. Antonio de Lancastre?

After your return we must arrange a number of things, especially in the matter of lists. We must obtain subscriptions from Spain: up to the present, as far as I know, King Alfonso has done nothing in spite of his promise! Do you think it worth while for me to write to him? I am delighted that you have obtained the three volumes of the *Ordenações* which were lacking and that you have also obtained an option on volumes three and four of the *Vita Christi* in case mine do not arrive: as for the *Gil Vicente* I am enormously interested in this. We must go full steam ahead to obtain subscriptions: as you most certainly understand it is difficult for me to ask for them *personally*. . . .

You have won your bet. . . . On the morning of the 24th I handed over the first five manuscripts complete, both in Portuguese and in English, revised, etc. They comprise the *De Bello Septense;* the Miniature of the Infanta Dona Isabella, Duchess of Burgundy; the *Ben Nahman;* the *Abudrahim;* and the *Vita Christi*. The latter comprises 30 pages in Portuguese and about the same number of pages

* Ayres d'Ornellas, King Manuel's representative in Portugal, died in Lisbon, December 14th, 1930.

in English!! I think it is the most complete and most interesting essay I have written. But what a work! I confess that I am very tired, having worked during the last eight days an average of 9½ hours a day: Miss Withers remained one evening until 11 o'clock!

But it gives me confidence to know that I am now "in the printers' hands"! I am taking a rest of three or four days so as to be able to attend to my correspondence which has been much delayed; after that I shall make a fresh start: I should have five more manuscripts ready by the end of January: the *Kaminto* is done, but two of them will be hard going: the *Marco Polo* and the *Autos dos Apostolos.*

What I would like to know is if my books [from the Ajuda Library] are coming and when. The Ambassador has again written to Dr. Júlio Dantas: it is so important for me to know if the books will soon be sent.

After this new lot of five manuscripts my work will be easier, for I have quite a number which are already ready and I could then supply Morrison [Stanley Morrison]* with a greater number of them.

I have not seen the "Dummy"!

I must tell you that Miss Withers has been wonderful; without her I would never have been able to finish what I have just done. That is the news which I can give you:

At the end of the week I shall start my work

---

* The noted typographer, at that time consultant of the Cambridge University, also supervised the printing and design of King Manuel's monumental work.

again. Here it is again very cold: it has been snowing
for 24 hours and the snow is more than 20 centi-
meters deep!!

Please accept all my thanks and at the same time
my most sincere wishes for the New Year.

I beg you, my dear Dr. Ettinghausen, to believe
me,

Your very affectionate

MANUEL R.

Fulwell Park, Twickenham

31. XII. 1927

MY DEAR DR. ETTINGHAUSEN,

Thank you for your letter of the 27th. I hope you
have received my letter which I sent to Madrid as
well as my telegram in answer to yours. I am most
interested in all the news you have given me and
very grateful to you. As to No. 184, this seems very
curious! As to the mysterious book (No. 548), I
think that the copy I possess is *an edition other* than
that mentioned by Anselmo. My copy is *certainly*
printed at the beginning of the sixteenth century: if
548 was printed by João Fernandes it must have been
in 1578 or 1579. Moreover my copy is printed in
gothic types and João Fernandes printed in roman
and italic types. The "puzzle" is therefore all the
greater. As you know the British Museum did not
find or understand anything about this: it is an interesting matter for further study.

I have taken a few days' rest partly in order to be
able to write some dozens of letters. Tomorrow I

will start my work again . . . as to my books from
Lisbon (Ajuda) I have heard nothing new! Apparently an *unknown force* is necessary to make
them come!!! When will you be returning?

It has been snowing for a week. There have been
terrible storms of icy winds; the cold is intense;
during the last week the thermometer has remained
below Zero! No one *remembers* such intense cold in
England, and it seems that this will continue because this morning the thermometer showed 7 degrees below Zero!

My dear friend, all my very sincere and affectionate wishes for happiness in 1928: may the New Year
witness the triumph of our work!

Your very devoted

MANUEL R.

Fulwell Park,
Twickenham, Middx.
15. II. 1928

MY DEAR DOCTOR,

Herewith a manuscript to be typewritten: I beg
you to send it to me as soon as it is ready. Have you
any news of the books from Lisbon? . . . I have just
read the article in the *Times*. Excellent!

If you have been able to obtain any news or information about the *Zacuto* please let me hear from
you. If you have something for me you can give it
to the chauffeur.

Your very affectionate

MANUEL R.

Fulwell Park, Twickenham
9. XI. 1928

MY DEAR DR. ETTINGHAUSEN,

I have received your letter and pages 521–568 of paged proof from Cambridge [University Press] . . . as soon as possible I will return them revised.

I have been thinking that the first volume of my book must soon come to an end. After careful examination of the problem, and having discussed it with Miss Withers, I came to the conclusion that some items intended to be published in the first volume of my book will have to be left out for the present, and published later in a supplement at the end of the last volume. Otherwise, the first volume would have more than 700 pages, and I feel I could not finish the work before a month, apart from writing the Introduction, which is, undoubtedly, most important.

I cannot deny that I am feeling the strain of the work and I consider that it is necessary that the first volume of my book should be published as soon as possible. . . . I am then proposing that I should write [on] three more books . . . at the end of which I shall write *Laus Deo!* If I had still to write about the other books, it would mean another month's work at least; and then I should have to write the Introduction which must be written when I am absolutely free from the other work. The revision of proofs is a tiring job too, and must be done most carefully. . . .

Believe me, my dear Dr. Ettinghausen,

Yours very sincerely,

MANUEL R.

Appendix

> Fulwell Park, Twickenham
> 22. XII. 1928

DEAR DOCTOR,

Herewith the mountain of proofs which I have here plus the additional corrections of the *Regra dos Monges.* . . .

I am also sending you the beautiful and precious *Foral* of Dom Manuel to be handed to Morrison, in which he will find not only the coat-of-arms of Dom Manuel but the exact colors, since it is a document signed by the fortunate King.

Bon voyage, a happy Xmas and New Year!

Give me news of anything you may find: *I beg you to be back in London before the 15th of January.*

I feel very tired, and really I need a holiday.

Thank you for everything and

> Believe me always
> Your devoted friend,
> MANUEL R.

> Palermo, Gd. Hôtel et des Palmes,
> 13. II. 1929

MY DEAR DOCTOR,

. . . The reproductions in red are superb, and I beg you to congratulate Mr. Morrison on my behalf. Please remember me to him.

All that I have received of the book seems to me excellent and I am *extremely satisfied:* the people to whom I have shown the sheets have found them superb. Many people have asked me for news of the book beginning with the Crown Prince of Italy.

205

. . . I am very happy to hear that Mr. Morrison is not going to America: this reassures me because otherwise, as *you* are going, I would be very anxious. I should very much like to receive soon the large woodcut coat-of-arms and to see the block (reproduction, of course) for the cover.

The news you sent me about the *Gil Vicente* made my mouth water!!! You can imagine how anxious I am to see that magnificent copy of such a rare and important book! I cannot help saying how sorry I am that you shall not be able to stay long enough in England to see the whole of the proofs through the Press; but I think and hope no more difficulties will arise. . . .

With every possible good wish for a happy journey to America and my grateful thanks for your invaluable help, believe me

Your devoted friend,
Manuel R.

Cannes, Grand Hôtel
3. III. 1950

My dear Dr. Ettinghausen,

. . . I have come here from Rome extremely worn out. . . . I was therefore absolutely in need of a rest and afterwards (as happens every year when I am here) I suffered from a sharp attack of epistolary laziness which it is very difficult for me to shake off! Again I must beg you . . . to excuse my silence.

When I shall have the pleasure of seeing you I shall tell you of my long conversation with His

Holiness: you would have been happy to listen to what the Holy Father told me about Volume I of my book!!! I would be afraid of blushing if I were to repeat to you the Pope's words.

. . . As I telegraphed you I was delighted to get your good news about the *Ordenações* of Dom Manuel (1512–1513). You are really an extraordinary person! Moreover you also tell me that you have other surprises: what are they? I am impatient to hear of them, as you can imagine.

I hope you are well . . . and beg you, my dear Doctor, to believe me always

Your devoted friend,

MANUEL R.

Index